Raiders Overhead

by

Stephen Flower

Air Research Publications

First published 1994 by
Air Research Publications
PO Box 223, Walton-on-Thames,
Surrey, KT12 3YQ,
England.

Typeset in Great Britain by
A.C.E.Services
Radlett, Herts. WD7 8LU

Printed in Great Britain by
MBA Group Ltd
London N17 0HW

ISBN 1-871187-18-4

Raiders Overhead

The German Air Operations

Over the Weybridge Area

in

Two World Wars

By

Stephen Flower

CONTENTS

Appendices

BROOKLANDS 1940

When home on leave from Larkhill that September
They came in fast and low and I remember
Saying to Mother, 'Are you short of butter?'
Talking across the coffee - then the stutter
Of a strident Bofors, out of context there
And I bemused push back my breakfast chair,
Dash to the orchard, looking up at those
Departing wings, twin engines and short nose.
With confidence cry out, 'Six Blenheims, dear, our crates.'
But quickly tell myself they're not, they're 88s.
I should have known, for only yesterday
I'd come from Waterloo and they
The Luftwaffe, had pushed a daylight raid
Right up the Portsmouth line and made
Our train pull up at Surbiton in flames
Near misses making fountains in the Thames.
Now urgently the phone sounds in the hall
Calling all volunteers to Weybridge Hospital.
'They're bombing Brooklands,' Mother's quote.
She backs the Morris Oxford down the drive,
'Look in the larder, won't be back till five.'
The Spits caught two, I think, the Hurriboxes
Too slow to catch hedge-hopping German foxes.

This poem was written by Roger Cobley, a young Territorial Army artillery officer, who was at home on leave at St George's Hill, Weybridge, on 4th September 1940. His mother, a local Red Cross volunteer, did not return home until nearly midnight.

Foreword

This book tells the story of the effects of two World Wars in the air as far as the Walton and Weybridge district of Surrey was concerned. Details from various official records have been combined with eye-witness accounts. Just about every incident arising from enemy action or presence, whose details are known and for which a date can be found, has been included, although it cannot be said that this account includes everything that occurred. Also included are details of air battles by day and night that took place over or close to this area. Where German aircraft are said to have been claimed shot down, this indicates that so far no definite proof of their loss has come to light, although such claims were no doubt made in good faith at the time.

To avoid ambiguity, especially where events were spread overnight, the 24-hour clock has been used in most instances. Anyone using a current map or Surrey A-Z will see that some of the streets and places mentioned have changed spellings or names. Those that were correct at the time have been used here.

Although this book is aimed at aircraft enthusiasts and at those who today live in the Weybridge area, I hope it will be of wider interest, as an illustration of how one area coped with the demands of total war. If it encourages people, wherever they may live, to take more interest in their local history, then its purpose will have been served.

Stephen Flower.

May 1993.

Bibliography

Twenty-Five Years at Brooklands. R L Beauchamp.

The Air Defence of Great Britain 1914-18. Christopher Cole and E F Cheesman.

Wings Over Brooklands. Howard Johnson.

Battle Over Britain. Francis K.Mason.

Strike from the Sky. Alexander McKee.

Zeppelins Over England. Kenneth Poolman.

The Battle of Britain Then and Now. Edited by Winston Ramsay.

The Blitz Then and Now, Volumes 1-3. Edited by Winston Ramsay.

The Rise and Fall of the Third Reich. William L Shirer.

The World of Wings and Things. Sir Alliott Verdon Roe.

Bombsights Over England. John J Vasco.

Acknowledgements

This short account of the effects of two World Wars on the Walton and Weybridge district came about as the result of my research into the wartime history of Brooklands airfield and the companies that were based there at the time. A check at Elmbridge Museum resulted in the Council records for this period coming to light. Considering the circumstances under which they were compiled, they were surprisingly detailed and formed a primary source of reference, especially for raids during the latter part of 1940. I wish to thank Avril Lansdell, her successor April Whincop, and their staff for their patient assistance. Miss Peggy Millson's account of her experiences as an air-raid warden, and Mr W H Askew's story of the first V-1 incident at Walton also came from this source.

My thanks are also due to Julian Temple, the Aviation Curator at Brooklands Museum, for his support and suggestions, and the staff of the Public Record Office at Kew. Mr Gerard Sutton of the Royal Artillery Library at Woolwich provided much useful information concerning units of Anti-Aircraft Command, and John Vasco, who has extensively researched the history of the Luftwaffe's specialist fighter-bomber unit, *Erprobungsgruppe 210*, was most helpful in supplying details of the two raids that this unit took part in over Brooklands during September 1940. Further information on the *Steinbock* raids of early 1944 was located with the assistance of Renata Hutton-Mills of Elmbridge Borough Council. Simon Parry, my publisher and a fellow aircraft enthusiast, also read the manuscript and made many useful suggestions, which resulted in a much improved final draft.

However, I feel that the chief honours must go to the wartime witnesses, whose surprisingly vivid memories of events which took place over half a century ago gave the story a flavour it would otherwise have lacked, and who, by means of interviews or correspondence, patiently answered the many questions I had to ask. I am grateful to them all.

Stephen Flower.

Chapter One

In The Beginning

Mention the town of Weybridge to most people in southeast England and they will dismiss it as just another leafy commuter suburb in that belt of them that surrounds London. Mention Brooklands as well and they'll say, 'Oh, yes, wasn't there once a racetrack there?' Indeed there was, and it might surprise them to know that the expanse of grass in its centre was once just as significant as the banked concrete track that ran around the outside.

The bowl-shaped piece of land known as Brooklands formed part of the estate of a wealthy Surrey landowner, the Honourable Hugh Fortescue Locke King. A car enthusiast and a patriotic individual, Locke King had gone to Italy in the early 1900s when a car race, the Targa Florio, had been staged through the streets of the town of Brescia. He had been dismayed to find that no British cars had been competing and his mood did not improve when the Italians told him that there were no British cars capable of taking part in such events. Determined to provide a circuit to both test and race cars, Locke King hired some 2,000 navvies from as far away as Yorkshire and Ireland. These men came to Surrey and began work around the clock in August 1906. Amid scenes reminiscent of the Railway Mania of the 1840s, they diverted the river Wey, which had meandered through the site. They also demolished some thirty acres of woodland and built an oval circuit measuring two and three-quarter miles around its circumference. Much of the circuit was banked to allow for negotiating curves at speeds of up to 120 miles per hour.

It was the first purpose-built banked motor-racing track in the world and it aroused some very mixed feelings, especially during the first race meeting on 6th July 1907. The spectators marvelled at this new creation and the machines that snarled round it, while some nearby residents complained about the noise and eventually sought an injunction to close it down - without success. Had they known what was to follow in 1940 they would have had even more reason to object.

Among those who attended the first race meeting was one Alliott Verdon Roe, a young man with an ambition to fly. He had been told that during the early hours of the morning a period of freak still air could be found in the valley in which the track lay. While others watched the racing, Roe studied the grass in the centre. There were still some trees on it, particularly at the Byfleet end, but it looked just the place to test a new flying machine, especially as such engines as were available were unreliable and control in flight was tenuous.

Within a few weeks Roe had persuaded E de Rodakowski, the Clerk of the Course, to allow him to put up a small aircraft shed at his own expense and test fly, but only in the mornings, when no-one was about. Few people in Britain considered flying to have any future. Despite the exploits of the Wright brothers in the United States there were still those who believed that heavier-than-air flight was impossible. However, some motorists were sympathetic and agreed to tow Roe's biplane in short hops along the track's Finishing Straight. This was one of the few level parts of it and, given the wild and marshy ground in the centre, probably the only place at Brooklands that he could have flown from at that time. J T C Moore-Brabazon, another would-be pilot, joined Roe, but left soon afterwards for Eastchurch on the Isle of Sheppey.

Roe lived a lonely and depressing life on five shillings' worth of food a week, sleeping illegally in his shed to take full advantage of the early morning air, and suffering trouble with, among other things, propeller blades breaking off. Then, on 8th June 1908, while taxiing along the straight on his own, he suddenly realized that he was flying at last! This lasted a few seconds, covering a hundred and fifty feet. It was the first powered and 'controlled' heavier-than-air flight by a native-born Englishman, although it was not recognized as such for twenty years. The credit initially went to Moore-Brabazon, who made his first flight at Eastchurch in the autumn of the following year. Controversy over Roe's feat continues to this day, although it can certainly be said that this was the start of aviation at Brooklands.

However, Rodakowski and the Committee members of the Brooklands Automobile Racing Club had little time for aspiring aviators and Roe was compelled to move on. Flying might not have resumed at Brooklands if it had not been for the publicity generated by two French aviators. One was Louis Bleriot, who became famous for the first powered flight across the English Channel in 1909. Suddenly the sea was no longer the secure barrier it had once been. It was pointless Britannia continuing to rule the waves if the skies were to become freely available. A single aeroplane today - and perhaps an invading airborne army tomorrow? There was also the question of national prestige. This might be the era of the *entente cordiale*, but what was a Frenchman doing flying over the English Channel? Nevertheless, Bleriot was seen as a hero in both countries and the official British attitude to flying began to change. The era of the solitary aviator, until now regarded as a crank, was ending.

That year there was a change of heart at Brooklands as well. George Holt Thomas, whose family owned the Graphic newspaper, had seen the performance of another aviation pioneer, Louis Paulhan, at an aeronautical meeting near Rheims. Sensing that aviation was the coming thing, Thomas quickly engaged Paulhan and then persuaded Locke King to allow the central area of Brooklands to be used for a flying display.

Within a few weeks Paulhan had performed at the track before a considerable crowd, and it was sufficient to encourage Locke King to set up a permanent airfield there. Major Lindsay Lloyd, who had replaced Rodakowski as Clerk of the Course, was far more sympathetic to the idea of flying than his predecessor. Realising the potential that flying had as a means of attracting the public to Brooklands, quite apart from enhancing Britain's standing in the world, Lindsay Lloyd hired more labourers to fell the remaining trees at the Byfleet end of the track. He then built a row of twelve sheds there for aviators to hire. No longer an outcast, Roe returned to Brooklands, to take up residence in new and larger premises.

This was the start of an era that was later summed up in the film *Those Magnificent Men In Their Flying Machines*. It was a time when aviation combined with the racing events to provide exciting and daring spectacles at Brooklands. Locke King's venture now seemed certain to prosper, but there was a cloud on the horizon that no-one had foreseen. The first primitive reconnaissance and bombing aircraft took to North African skies during the Italo-Turkish conflict of 1911-12, proving to anyone with eyes to see that they and their more powerful successors would have a role to play in any future conflict.

It was not long before some enterprising Service officers began to take an interest in what was happening at Brooklands, and Captain JB Fulton of the Royal Artillery flew a Deperdussin aircraft that Roe had modified. Fulton later played a prominent part in the setting-up of the British Army's Air Battalion in March 1911, which led the following year to the establishment of the Royal Flying Corps. This was organised as a corps within the Army, with similar status to the Royal Engineers - and indeed many sappers were to join the new squadrons as they formed.

Other uniforms and pilots began to be seen on the airfield. Thomas Sopwith, already a noted balloonist and yachtsman, had quickly mastered the rudiments of airmanship at Brooklands by teaching himself to fly in just one day. Soon afterwards he found himself giving instruction to a certain Major Hugh Trenchard. Trenchard would later go on to command the Royal Flying Corps and be the first Chief of the Air Staff of the Royal Air Force when it was founded in April 1918.

In the summer of 1914 a large-scale troop exercise took place in Surrey. On Saturday 20th June senior Army officers and members of the Royal Family witnessed an advance by 'enemy' troops whom, according to the exercise's scenario, had invaded southern England, with 'friendly' forces retreating across the airfield towards the bridge at Walton-on-Thames. RFC aircraft took the role of aerial scouts and the Brooklands Flying Village, as it had become known, became a temporary field hospital. Six weeks later, on 4th August, the games ceased and war was declared when German troops invaded Belgium.

For the first time since the Crimean conflict Britain was facing a European war and one of the questions was what part aircraft would play in it. Could they drop bombs with any real effect, could they fight one another, or would they turn out to be ill-suited to an all-out war, except for reconnaissance? Many early aviators, including Roe, had somewhat naively believed that aircraft could and should only be used for peaceful purposes. It was cruelly ironic that Roe should see the invention he had helped to develop now being used as a weapon of war - and one which one day would return to Surrey with an intent that was anything but peaceful. It must also have seemed strange to him later in life to see the Avro company - which had taken its name from his initials - go on to produce the Lancaster and the Vulcan - two of the most famous bombers the RAF would ever have. However, all this lay in a murky and uncertain future.

Chapter Two

Mathy's Raid

The same patriotic spirit that had inspired Locke King to build the track also led him to offer it to the Government on the outbreak of war. Within a day the RFC had taken over, designating the airfield an Aircraft Acceptance Park. Several new RFC squadrons would form there and basic flying training would be carried out. The racetrack was closed, although a couple of Forces motorcycle sprint events were held there in 1915. All usable aircraft were commandeered and the nearby Bleriot and Handasyde works, which had sprung up in the last years of peace, gave their full attention to military contracts. Products designed by the pioneers were soon in action, with Roe's Avro 504 and Sopwith's Tabloid going to France for reconnaissance and light bombing purposes.

The possibility of enemy aerial bombardment had not been overlooked and in October 1914 it had been agreed that it would be the duty of the Admiralty's Royal Naval Air Service to defend the London area. The RFC would assist ground forces should any enemy landings take place. However, any surplus RFC aircraft could co-operate with the RNAS in aerial defence. Besides training, the role of Brooklands would be to supply aircraft for defence elsewhere as necessary. The BE2C was an observation biplane produced by the Royal Aircraft Factory at Farnborough. It was slow and would soon be outclassed in France by the new and deadly Fokker monoplane. However, the inherent stability that had been built into it would accidentally result in an aircraft that was quite well suited to the task of hunting Germany's Zeppelin airships.

Quiet, cigar-like and sinister in appearance, the Zeppelin would come to symbolise the first air war over Britain, but it was German seaplanes that would make the first raid, dropping bombs in the sea off Dover on 21st December 1914. Two days before, Farnborough, Brooklands and Hounslow airfields had each been ordered to provide two aircraft to stand by over the Christmas period.

An unofficial truce reigned in the trenches on the Western Front that Christmas, but there was none at home. Shortly after noon on Christmas Day a German seaplane was seen off Sheerness and fired on by an anti-aircraft battery, but although an aircraft took off from Brooklands no interception was effected.

The first Zeppelin attack was by the airships L3 and L4, which on 19th January 1915 bombed coastal towns in East Anglia. During the spring of 1915 the station commander at Brooklands was one of several who were reminded to keep one aircraft always at readiness. The aircraft were to carry bombs and explosive darts - the idea being to fly above a Zeppelin and drop them on it! This was not quite as absurd as it sounded, for Sub-Lieutenant R A J Warneford of the RNAS had destroyed a Zeppelin over Ghent in Belgium by bombing it and had been awarded the Victoria Cross as a result. Machine guns were considered useless due to a lack of suitable ammunition. The Zeppelin carried hydrogen-filled gasbags within its alloy-framed hull and it was thought to also carry an inert gas that would mix with the hydrogen in case of a bag being pierced by a bullet. Later an RNAS officer, Squadron Commander F A Brock - of the famous family of firework makers - would devise an explosive bullet that, with tracer ammunition, would literally shoot this idea down in flames, but as yet no-one had realized how vulnerable Zeppelins would turn out to be.

On 8th September 1915 *Kapitänleutnant* Heinrich Mathy, who was to become one of the best-known of the Zeppelin commanders, attacked London, leaving the population at first frightened, then angry and demanding action. The bombs were accompanied by a note that stated, 'We have come and we will come again soon.' The writer meant what he said. Three more raids on the 11th, 12th and 13th underlined the urgency of the situation. Clearly Brooklands and Farnborough were too far to the west of London to meet this new threat, and other airfields were needed in Essex. Such an airfield was Sutton's Farm,

The Zeppelin L13, commanded by Kapitänleutnant Heinrich Mathy, which raided the Guildford area in October 1915. (IWM Q58456)

which as RAF Hornchurch would become famous in another much more desperate defence twenty-five years later. One pilot posted to it was Second Lieutenant John Slessor.

Slessor had trained on the French-designed Maurice Farman Longhorn biplane at Brooklands in 1915, and had then done thirty-five hours of solo flying on a variety of aircraft. He had crashed four of them and had come close to being dismissed from the training course. In October 1915 he had been assigned to Home Defence duties, flying a BE2C armed with eight twenty-pound bombs under the wings. On the night of 13th October he took off to intercept another raid, seeing a Zeppelin some four thousand feet above him as he climbed. Anti-aircraft fire burst near the airship and although the gunners' aim was inaccurate the German commander, *Kapitänleutnant* Breithaupt, was shaken and his airship climbed rapidly away. Having lost it in the clouds, Slessor turned for home and crashed when a searchlight crew, trying to illuminate the airfield's rudimentary flarepath, shone their light in his face as he landed. The BE2C finished up in a turnip field, with damage to the undercarriage and one wingtip.

Mathy, in the Zeppelin L13, was also over Essex that night, having taken off from his base at Hage at 13.40 hours that afternoon. Although disconcerted by the heavy fire directed at Breithaupt, Mathy did not panic and skirted London to the west as he had planned, with the waterworks at Hampton-on-Thames as his target. He was seen at Windsor, too far to the west of Hampton, and crossed the Thames near Weybridge at ten minutes to ten. Five minutes later he passed Effingham and headed west. Why there was no reaction from Brooklands is unknown, although possibly the order for one aircraft to be kept at readiness had by now been rescinded. At ten past ten Mathy reached Guildford, having dropped a flare near the village of East Clandon to find his position.

At this time British anti-aircraft defences were meagre, with most guns going to feed the demands of the Western Front. In this part of Surrey the only defence was a one-pounder gun at a gunpowder factory near Chilworth, southeast of Guildford. This weapon opened fire when Mathy dropped a second flare. He turned east, then back over the factory and Guildford, dropped a third flare and followed it with twelve high explosive bombs, which fell near the village of Shalford. Some of these damaged the London and South-Western Railway's main line between two tunnels just south of Guildford station.

On his way back to London, Mathy's Zeppelin passed its sister ship, the L14, commanded by *Kapitänleutnant* Aloys Böcker, near Caterham. Having come up from Edenbridge in Kent, the L14 had bombed the Croydon area, killing nine people, and then turned east, almost colliding with Mathy near Bromley. Böcker is said to have later complained about Mathy's navigation, which, given his unintended excursion over Surrey, does seem to have been of a low standard on this night. Nevertheless, Mathy headed northeast towards London, later bombing Woolwich barracks. The only fatality in the Guildford area that night was a swan, killed when two of the L14's bombs fell in the river Wey!

There was a second BE2C at Sutton's Farm, but it was useless as its bomb release gear had not yet been fitted. Slessor could only stand impotently on the airfield and watch as Mathy passed overhead. The 13th was a night of blunders on both sides.

Time passed and more Zeppelins were lost as the defenders gained experience. Mathy and his crew, who later transferred to the larger L31, fell victim to the tracer bullets of Second Lieutenant W J Tempest over Hertfordshire on 1st October 1916. Tempest barely managed to get out of the way as the entire Zeppelin caught fire and plunged to earth 'roaring like a furnace' near Potters Bar.

Later, Gotha and Giant bombers flew over London by day and night, the latter living up to their name with a wingspan greater than some later four-engined monoplanes. Mathy's raid of 1915, however, was the only one during the 1914-18 war to pose a threat to the Weybridge area. Had Mathy realized how close he had come to Brooklands he might well have decided to drop his entire load on it.

So the first major war in the air dragged on, like that in the trenches below, ending with a victory that seemed hollow when the last of the long casualty lists came in. Of the young daredevils who had delighted the pre-war crowds at Brooklands, and of the earnest boys in uniform who had come to train there, few, as little as one in twenty, ever returned.

Chapter Three
First Blood

So 1918 ended and the war to end all wars, or so it was thought, began to recede into history. Brooklands slowly came back to life, racing resumed in 1920 and former Service pilots tried to find a new use for their skills by giving 'five bob' trips from the airfield. The Vickers company had occupied the former Itala motor repair works on the southeast side of the track since 1915. It now produced the Vimy bomber, a modified version of which made headlines when John Alcock and Arthur Whitten-Brown made the first successful nonstop aerial crossing of the Atlantic in it during 1919. Several different flying clubs formed at Brooklands and a club building was built for them in 1932 at the Flying Village.

Flying was beginning to shrink the world, but despite its increasing respectability many companies in the aviation industry lived on what seemed a hand-to-mouth basis. The peacetime RAF, and the Fleet Air Arm, which it then controlled, needed only a few new aircraft. To keep going and retain some of its work force Vickers produced a string of unrelated products, among them children's toys, concrete mixers and a strange item called the Guinea Gramophone.

The Sopwith Company went into voluntary liquidation in 1920 while still solvent, and out of it was to come the Hawker Engineering Company, named after the pioneering test pilot Harry Hawker. This company would be renamed Hawker Aircraft Limited in 1934 and its Chief Designer, Sydney Camm, would produce a famous series of fighters and light bombers that would serve the RAF and many foreign air forces for over six decades. Although Hawker aircraft were manufactured at Kingston, they were transported to Brooklands by road, either partly assembled or as kits of parts, to be put together and flown out from the airfield. Up to 1939 all the Hawker prototypes, from one-off aircraft like the Hoopoe to the famous

Brooklands, photographed from the south in the mid-thirties, during a flying display. The then-new Hawker assembly shed can be seen beside the race-track. The Flying Village is immediately behind and the Vickers factory is in the right background. (Brooklands Museum)

Hart series of multi-role biplanes, first took to the air from Brooklands. Eventually the demand for Hawker products outstripped the limited facilities there and the company moved to Langley in Buckinghamshire. In 1934 a distinctive long assembly shed, slightly 'kinked' to fit into the available space, was built for Hawkers at the Byfleet end of the track, replacing the earlier line of sheds used by Roe, Sopwith and others.

By 1935 the threat posed by Nazi Germany was becoming apparent, especially when that country's Chancellor, Adolf Hitler, and his friend, former fighter pilot Hermann Göring, publicly announced the existence of their new air force, the *Luftwaffe*. They boasted that its strength already equalled that of the RAF. Belatedly Britain began to rearm, the Air Ministry issuing several new specifications for monoplane fighters and bombers. In November 1935 the Hawker Hurricane fighter first flew at Brooklands, to be followed in June 1936 by the B9/32, the prototype Vickers Wellington bomber. Production of both types began during the final months of 1937, their sombre camouflaged shapes making a sinister contrast with the silver-doped biplanes that had preceded them.

In October 1938 the Munich Crisis erupted when Hitler demanded that the Sudetenland, a German-speaking part of Czechoslovakia, be incorporated within Germany's borders. Europe held its breath while the fate of this 'far-off' country was decided. Brooklands had been earmarked as a possible RAF fighter airfield in times of emergency, and Auxiliary Air Force reservists found themselves reporting to the Barrage Balloon Centre at nearby Hook. Finally Britain's Prime Minister, Neville Chamberlain, came home proclaiming peace, while glossing over the fact of having abandoned Czechoslovakia to the tender mercies of her Nazi neighbour. Most people relaxed - but not for long.

In the early spring of 1939 Hitler, despite having said that he had no further territorial demands to make in Europe, went on to occupy what was left of Czechoslovakia. By now convinced that Britain and France were too spineless to stop him, he then made various threats concerning his other eastern neighbour, Poland. War now seemed inevitable and few were surprised when Poland was invaded on 1st September 1939.

With recent wars in Spain and Ethiopia in mind - wars in which German and Italian bombers had played a prominent part - there was in Britain a strong fear of a massive aerial attack, possibly involving the use of poison gas. To mitigate whatever effects this form of warfare might have on the population, the ARP Organization had been set up in the late Thirties. On 1st September 1939 Miss Peggy Millson, an ARP warden at Weybridge, was ordered to organize a rough rota of wardens, and their posts were quickly manned. It was a Friday morning, and while the *Luftwaffe* dive-bombers screamed through Polish skies Surrey's pin-striped commuters were calmly making their way to work as usual. Standing there on duty with her white warden's armband plainly visible, she began to feel ridiculous as the sirens remained silent, especially as some people passing knew her.

The interior of the Hawker shed shortly before the outbreak of war. Harry Patrick, the assistant Works Manager (at left) watches as his force tackles one of the first batches of Hurricanes. (Hawker Aircraft Company 761808 via A.E. Tagg and Brooklands Museum)

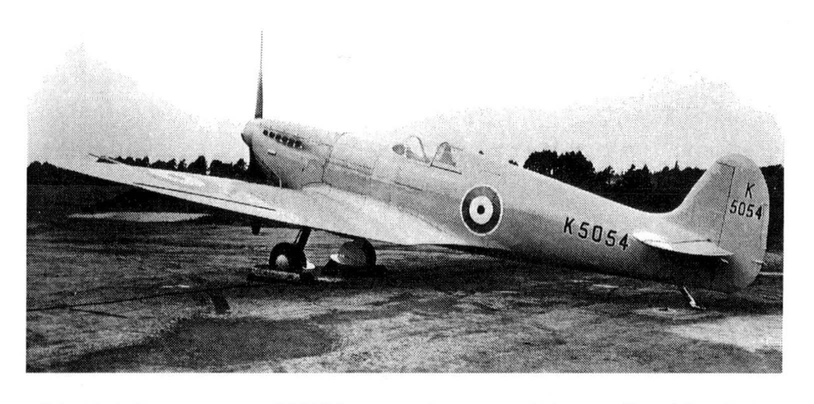

The Spitfire prototype K5054 was a frequent visitor to Brooklands in the late thirties. (IWM MH5214)

The weekend came and fighting in Poland continued, although the Surrey skies remained ominously quiet. On Sunday morning an announcement was made by the BBC that the Prime Minister would broadcast to the nation at 11.15. Those who lacked 'the wireless' were invited into the homes of others - in some instances for the first time. Preparations for the ritual of Sunday lunch were interrupted by the tired and rueful voice of Neville Chamberlain.

> "I am speaking to you from the Cabinet Room at 10 Downing Street. This morning the British Ambassador in Berlin handed the German Government a final Note, stating that unless we heard from them by eleven o'clock that they were prepared at once to withdraw their troops from Poland, a state of war would exist between us. I have to tell you now that no such undertaking has been received, and that consequently this country is at war with Germany......We and France are today, in pursuit of our obligations, going to the aid of Poland, who is so bravely resisting this wicked and unprovoked attack on her people."

Peggy Millson had been on duty since seven o'clock that morning and had strained to catch the news from radio sets she could hear nearby. Hearing enough to know that the war had begun, she felt a sense of shock. 'Everyone I met later in the day seemed to be suffering from this heavy dullness.' The only words to pass between her and her relief were, 'It's happened.'

The Sunday morning silence now seemed even more threatening, but it was abruptly shattered as the sirens wailed just after 11.30. Cursing Hitler for wasting no time, the off-duty wardens dashed back to their posts and waited for the long-anticipated aerial holocaust. Still nothing happened. This first alert was a false alarm, though it gave more than a hint of what was to come.

It was the start of that strange period known as the 'Phoney War'. Ration coupons were doled out, gas masks were carried but seldom worn and cars were laid up for want of petrol. The war reached Surrey's citizens only via the Press, radio and newsreels. Any aircraft seen overhead were likely to be from Brooklands, and soon that airfield's products were in action, though not yet in their home skies. In December 1939 twenty-four Wellingtons, representing three RAF squadrons, set out to attack any German naval vessels they could find near the port of Wilhelmshaven. They were spotted by an early German

The defenders. An AFS fire crew and their trailer pump at Elm Grove, Walton, circa 1939. (Elmbridge Museum 300. 1989/1)

radar set and as a result lost over half their number to heavy fighter opposition.

Another Wellington droned over Weybridge with a strange hoop-like device fitted beneath it. This, known only to a few Vickers staff, carried an electric current to explode a new menace at sea - the German magnetic mine. Hurricanes flew convoy patrols off the east coast, where on 21st October a group of minelaying He115s were caught by pilots of 46 Squadron. Five Heinkels were claimed destroyed, the first confirmed victories for Hurricanes. A few days later, on 30th October, Hurricanes of the the British Expeditionary Force in France scored, when Pilot Officer P W O Mould of 1 Squadron scored this squadron's first victory - a Dornier 17P reconnaissance bomber.

Heavy 3.7-inch guns arrived in the Weybridge area, deploying at Fairmile Common, Wisley Common, Dunford Bridge and Woburn Park, near Addlestone. Lewis machine gun posts ringed Brooklands, but all the gunners could do was wait, while trying to keep warm through a particularly harsh winter. Their troubles did not end when the snow finally thawed, for the Wey went into full spate and flooded a gun post that had been sited too close to it. Bofors guns arrived at Brooklands in April 1940, but still the war was happening elsewhere.

Suddenly things began to speed up as Hitler launched the first phase of his offensive in the west, with successful attacks on Denmark and Norway. German aerial activity began to increase and Weybridge received its first, almost unseen, visit from the Luftwaffe.

27th April 1940

An aircraft of uncertain identity, listed as Raid X49, was plotted by an RDF site at 16.32 hours off Lowestoft. It turned into the Thames estuary and followed the north bank of the river, flying over London and heading west at between 12,000 and 16,000 feet. At 17.15 hours it turned south near Reading and crossed the coast near Shoreham. Two gun sites in the London area caught sight of this aircraft in poor visibility and said it was a Heinkel 111, although the Observer Corps post at Weybridge identified it as a Junkers 88. Twelve RAF fighters were sent up, but there were no interceptions. X49's purpose and identity remain unknown, although it was probably a reconnaissance.

On 10th May the Phoney War abruptly ended when a major German offensive began in western Europe. Within six weeks France and Belgium had capitulated and what remained of the British Expeditionary Force had come home via Dunkirk or the other Channel ports. An invasion of Britain was now likely, and in common with the rest of the country the Brooklands aircraft companies formed Home Guard units in readiness.

Ted Petty was a fitter, employed on the production of Wellington wing spars at this time, and at twenty was a younger member of the Vickers Home Guard battalion.

> "You led a very unreal life. Some of the greatest fun I had was when I joined the Home Guard. I was fortunate enough to get into the armoured division."

Despite its grand title, this was only a small unit, equipped with Beaverette armoured cars and an old tank, in which some hilarious drives were staged around St. George's Hill, near the factory, under the direction of test pilot Jeffrey Quill.

A 3.7 inch gun ready to fire. Spare ammunition is stacked in boxes around the gun pit and ready-use shells can be seen on the left.
(IWM H25404)

Although keen to join the RAF, Ted was unable to do so for medical reasons, quite apart from working in a 'protected' industry, in which he was directed to remain.

> "We had a gun pit near the Clubhouse, lined with sandbags. We had six Bren guns and also twin Brownings from aircraft."

In 1940 many a Home Guard unit, and not a few Army ones, would have envied such firepower, but then Vickers were in a good position to get it.

> "When a Wellington came in for servicing - they used to come in with about two crews aboard - 'Mutt' Summers, the Chief Test Pilot, used to say, 'Do you want lunch? Right. That'll be 2,000 rounds of ammo!'"

Summers used to scrounge guns in the same way, persuading returning crew members to sign for the guns in their aircraft's turrets, even though that Wellington was actually about to leave Brooklands unarmed! However, this illegal weaponry was soon put to good use.

> "We had six twin Brownings on the roof on the Vickers office block, by Brooklands Road, and they were credited with one aircraft, which crashed over near Dorking."

There is some doubt as to the identity of this aircraft, although it may have been a Ju88 that attacked the factory the following October.

On 27th May a new weapon came to Brooklands - the Parachute-and-Cable installation. Manned by an RAF detachment, who were quartered in a large house nearby, this Heath Robinson-like device consisted of six rockets, which were fired from projectors on the ground. Attached to each rocket was a 480-foot length of one-ton steel cable with a 38-inch parachute at each end. At the top of the rocket's trajectory the cable was released and the parachute at the top opened, suspending the cable in the air. When hit by a low-flying aircraft's wing the second parachute would deploy at the bottom of the cable, exerting two tons of drag. If it struck the wing at the right angle it could pull the aircraft out of the sky.

This detachment, under the command of a corporal, was positioned near the notorious Brooklands sewage farm, near the Flying Village hangars. More will be said of this location later, but, given the fine weather for much of that summer, it must have been a most unpopular posting!

These weapons were also installed at many RAF bases, including the fighter airfields at Croydon and Kenley. They were first used against a low-level raid on Kenley on 18th August, bringing down a Do17Z. The disadvantage of the rockets and cables was that they could only reach up to 600 feet, and were therefore useless against attackers who came in above that height.

It is a measure of how desperate the situation had suddenly become that the Brooklands detachment was at first made up of men who had 'trained' in just two days for this role. In July the training course became four days, and, much later, three weeks!

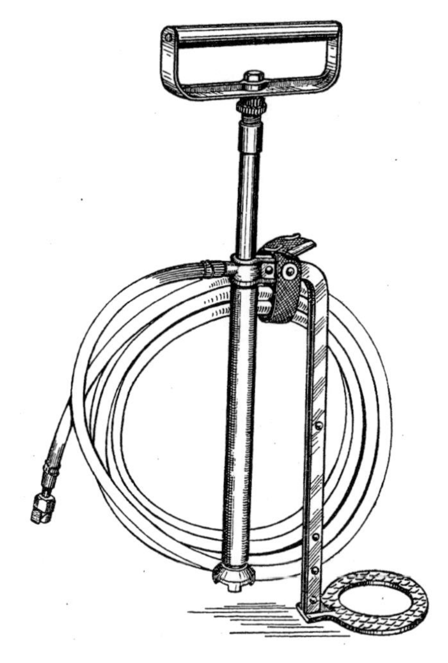

Practically every family had its own device for dealing with the expected incendiary bombs - a stirrup pump. It was designed to deliver around three gallons of water in two minutes with a jet some thirty feet in radius.

19th July 1940

At 07.03 hours a Dornier 17 crossed the coast near Eastbourne, flew over Brooklands and Croydon to within three miles of the RAF fighter base at Northolt, then returned via the same route.

20th July 1940

Raid UB7H (a classification meaning unidentified but believed hostile), reported as either an He111 or a Do17, was seen going north at 06.30 hours and was engaged by the Fairmile Common gun site when flying south twelve minutes later. This aircraft was chased by five Spitfires and was erroneously reported as having been shot down off Worthing.

24th July 1940

At 14.29 hours a raid was plotted by RDF south of the Isle of Wight. A Do17 flew east, crossed the coast near Angmering in Sussex and later appeared over Kingston, Chertsey and Wimbledon before flying south to cross the coast near Brighton.

This was the first air raid to be specifically directed at Brooklands, and the first incident of this kind to occur in the Weybridge area. RDF plots were passed to the Operations Room at Fighter Command, which in turn passed them on to its Group, Sector and Gun Operations Rooms, in this case to one at Weybridge, which passed it to the local gun positions. A series of contradictory plots was given, suggesting confusion over this aircraft's identity. The final one, stating it to be hostile, reached the guns at 15.19 hours. While all this was going on the Dornier had been circling Brooklands for several minutes at 4,000 feet, but visibility was bad, with heavy rain and clouds.

What happened next was witnessed by Jan Jacobs, then a 12-year old schoolboy living at Pinewood Avenue in New Haw.

> "I was coming home from Clark's College, a school in Surbiton. I got off the train at West Weybridge station (renamed Byfleet and New Haw in 1961) and I was in the open on the down platform when I heard a single shot from the ground. I looked up to see a shape dodging in and out of the clouds. About fifteen minutes later I was on the canal bank by the White Hart pub and I saw it again clearly."

Although he did not join the Air Training Corps until 1943, like many boys in the area Jan was an aircraft enthusiast, and recognized the intruder by the slim fuselage that gave it its nickname.

> "I remember thinking, 'A Flying Pencil'. This was definitely a Do 17P - not the later hammer-headed Z type. I'd walked along the road to New Haw Lock and I was just crossing the bridge near the White Hart when the attack started. The Dornier flew west to east, across my line of vision, and then all hell broke loose. I can remember the Bofors guns firing at it, and bombs falling out of the belly."

The single ineffective shot Jan had heard had come from the Fairmile Common gun site, which had glimpsed the intruder at 15.09 hours. Ten minutes later the bomber was seen again, but there were several training aircraft also flying around the area, complicating the gunners' task. Finally the Dornier came out of clouds at about 1,000 feet, north of the airfield, following two new and unarmed Wellingtons that were preparing to land after test flights. Lacking a rearward lookout, the Vickers test pilots would not have seen the danger behind. As they lowered their wheels the German craftily did the same, then suddenly changed course to fly over the Vickers works, aiming a stick of

A cheap and effective method of air-raid protection was the government designed Anderson Shelter. It was a pit, covered with interlocking sections of 'U' shaped corrugated iron, then protected with at least fifteen inches of earth. Thousands of these shelters were contructed, many in the gardens of houses. They proved remarkably effective against both blast and falling debris.

bombs at it.

A Bofors mounted on a tower on Members' Hill, overlooking the airfield, opened fire, but rain caused several of its shells to burst prematurely. The Dornier then flew back across the airfield towards the Hawker shed, strafing a gun site and a Wellington on the ground en route. Caught out in the open was Bill Wright, a sergeant in the Vickers Home Guard, who had been in a Beaverette armoured car at the time. Hastily abandoning his vehicle, he leapt into a nearby gun pit for safety, only to find that someone else had already got there. That someone turned out to be none other than Barnes Wallis, then the Chief Designer of Structures at Vickers, and responsible for the intricate geodetic design of the Wellington. While the alert remained in force Wallis spent some time telling Wright how he had come to design this aircraft!

A second stick of bombs from the Dornier missed Hawkers and a third stick landed in Walton. The Dornier and its enterprising crew then escaped.

Eighteen bombs had been dropped in all, of which five had struck the Brooklands track. Others, overshooting the Vickers works, had caused property damage on St. George's Hill to the south. Four men at Walton gasworks became casualties, and although one was detained in hospital overnight none was seriously hurt.

There had been no warning - an indication of what was to come - and a further pointer to what lay ahead was also to be found on St. George's Hill. 47 Bomb Disposal Section of the Royal Engineers had the unenviable job of removing an unexploded 250-Kilo bomb from this area. The section's commanding officer, Second Lieutenant How-White, defused the bomb, which was later placed in his unit's storeroom at Reading until a suitable place could be found to blow it up. Meanwhile, although the explosive filling was retained, the bomb was used for unit instruction!

On 12th August a new Gun Operations Room at Datchet, near Windsor, replaced that at Weybridge. The light anti-aircraft detachments at Brooklands were connected by landline to the nearest heavy gun site, which would pass on any information intended for them. This arrangement was hardly perfect, but it was an improvement on what had gone before. The communications lag on the 24th had been noted, but evidently the lesson was not properly learned, for an even worse one would soon occur.

On the same day an unseen Luftwaffe aircraft flew over Brooklands to photograph the Hawker assembly shed, so adding this to a dossier on this area that included the Vickers factory and the Airscrew Howden works near Addlestone. The Hawker shed had been involved in the final assembly of the prototype Hurricane in 1935. It was now a prime source of over half the front-line strength of Fighter Command, since for every two Spitfire squadrons there were at least three equipped with Hurricanes. Although by 1940 this shed was no longer the sole source of Hurricane production - they were also being built by

In addition to the Anderson shelter, for use well away from buildings, the government also produced the Morrison Shelter, in effect a steel cage, for use within the home. The steel construction gave good crush protection, while the occupants were, to a degree, protected from rubble and flying debris by the steel-mesh 'bars' around them.

three other factories in Britain and Canada - it remained an important target.

German fighter pilots did not usually rate the Hurricane very highly, but their bomber crews were telling a different story, for this fighter's concentrated eight-gun armament could wreak havoc in the cockpit of an He111, a Do17 or a Ju88. In the Battle of Britain it was bomber losses that would decide the issue, as it was pointless for the Luftwaffe fighters to gain air superiority if in so doing their bomber force had become too depleted to take advantage of it.

16th August 1940

The Airscrew Howden works, added to the Weybridge target map of the Luftwaffe during June, may have been the reason for an alert at Addlestone at 16.00 hours, followed by some damage and casualties in that area, although no-one at the local Woburn Park gun site appeared to have seen the aircraft responsible. At 17.20 hours the Weybridge guns engaged an He111, then a second one ten minutes later. The need for vigilance was again displayed, for there was no warning until 17.45 hours! Two Junkers 88s and another Heinkel followed this at 17.59 hours - fire on the latter being hampered by cloud. A fourth Heinkel was seen at 18.30 hours and took evasive action when it was fired on.

21st August 1940

Fifteen bombs were dropped on Wisley Common at 21.30 and 22.30 hours, followed by three others at Addlestone at 23.14, causing little damage and no casualties. A further three bombs fell in the railway cutting between Weybridge and Walton. One failed to explode. At 23.30 hours four others fell on the Brooklands track, one damaging the nearby railway line.

23rd August 1940

Flares were dropped over Brooklands, but no bombs followed. This would happen several times in the months to come.

As the Battle of Britain raged over southern England and German bomber losses mounted, it became apparent to the *Luftwaffe* that daylight raids, even with increased fighter escort, were becoming too costly. For now they would continue, but night attacks had already been tried as an alternative and would now be steadily increased. One night in August an event took place that led to a complete change in the way that the battle was being fought. It was to relieve the pressure on Fighter Command, which besides losses in the air had sustained many severe attacks on its airfields.

24/25th August 1940

Several German bombers, detailed to bomb oil tanks on the Thames estuary, strayed over London and hit the East End, for the first time since 1918. Some aircraft were even further off course, as was shown by an He111 that, when illuminated by searchlights in the Guildford area, strafed two of their sites without effect. This bomber's target had been RAF Harwell in Oxfordshire, and as it returned it was shot down off Hastings by a Hurricane of 615 (County of Surrey) Squadron flown by Flight Lieutenant J G Sanders - one of very few RAF night victories at this time. At 21.35 hours flares again fell over Brooklands - evidently another lost pilot as no bombs immediately followed them.

Between 23.40 and 23.50 hours thirteen high explosive bombs fell in the Weybridge district, one demolishing a house at 43

A partially built Wellington in the Weybridge factory, awaiting its outer wings. On 4th September 1940 this factory would become the target for the Luftwaffe. (Brooklands Museum)

Normanhurst Road in Walton. The owners, both of whom were wardens, were away on duty at the time and their children, in the Anderson shelter in the back garden, were unharmed. One bomb hit another such shelter, killing a woman and wounding her husband. Another landed in the front gardens of two houses, blasting a crater twenty feet in diameter and ten feet deep. Ten others fell on open ground, although one hit Walton Boys' Central School, lodging in the roof. The resulting fire was controlled by wardens with a stirrup pump until the Fire Brigade arrived. There was a second raid in the small hours, and five unexploded bombs were later found in the area.

Still hoping for peace with Britain, Hitler had forbidden attacks on London. Once the mistake was realized, an investigation was conducted within the *Luftwaffe* to trace the bomber crews responsible, with the threat of a posting to an infantry regiment if they were traced.

25/26th August 1940

Göring's nose was put further out of joint when RAF Bomber Command raided Berlin as a reprisal. William L Shirer, an American journalist who would later write a famous history of Hitler's Third Reich, noted how stunned the Berliners were. This was not a completely new experience for them as one French naval aircraft had defiantly attacked Berlin on 7th June. However, this had hardly mattered when the French capitulation had followed two weeks later. The RAF raid caused no casualties, but the blow to German civilian morale was what mattered. Germans were not slow to see what mockery had been made of Göring's rash promise that such an event would never take place.

Wellingtons built at the Weybridge factory had taken part in this attack, and that night their home received further attention when more flares were dropped, followed by three bombs, between 21.35 and 21.40 hours. These fell in open country and did little damage.

29th August 1940

At 03.35 hours two HE bombs fell in the grounds of Whiteley Village, breaking several windows but doing no other damage. A small undergrowth fire was extinguished by an AFS pump. On the following evening an enemy aircraft circled Byfleet at 23.46 hours, dropping four bombs. One was an oil incendiary and failed to go off. Another was a delayed-action one, which finally exploded over nine hours later. There were no casualties, neither was any damage caused.

On the 31st things were quieter over Surrey. However, another former resident of Walton was to fight his last battle. Pilot Officer Raymond Aeberhardt was serving with 19 Squadron at RAF Fowlmere in Cambridgeshire. He was one of several pilots who intercepted an enemy force bombing the fighter base at RAF Debden in Essex. His Spitfire was damaged in the fight, forcing him to attempt a landing at Fowlmere without flaps. The fighter crashed and burnt out. He was killed at the age of nineteen.

While the night battle gathered momentum in early September, Göring ordered a change in *Luftwaffe* target policy for daylight raids. If bombing RAF fighter bases would not stem the flow of Hurricanes and Spitfires coming up to do battle, then the only alternative was to attack Britain's aircraft factories, to stop that flow at its source. This new policy was implemented from 4th September onwards. The *Luftwaffe* was about to return to Brooklands in force, and those who witnessed the next raid on the airfield there would never forget it.

Chapter Four
Target Brooklands

Formed from the RAF's Air Defence of Great Britain organization in 1936, Fighter Command had been split into four Groups. No.10 Group covered the west country, No.11 Group the southeast, No.12 Group the Midlands and No.13 Group the north. All had a part to play in Britain's defence, but as the Germans now occupied bases near the Channel coast it was inevitable that No.11 Group would receive the brunt of any attacks, most of which were now taking place over Kent and Sussex. Air Vice Marshal Sir Keith Park, commanding No.11 Group, often needed reinforcements, and Air Vice Marshal Sir Christopher Brand of No.10 Group readily provided them. On 4th September his support would be particularly welcome, as one of Brand's squadrons would indirectly take part in the defence of Brooklands. In 1920, as a young officer in the South African Air Force, Brand, with Lieutenant-Colonel Pierre van Ryneveld, had been one of the first airmen to fly from Brooklands to Cape Town, using two Vickers Vimys and a 'borrowed' De Havilland DH9A in a relay fashion. Both had received knighthoods as a result.

If Brand had flown over Brooklands in 1940 he might have had difficulty recognizing it again. The racetrack had of course closed again - this time for good, although no-one knew that yet - and the concrete surface, where suitable, was being used to park Wellingtons. The Vickers staff had camouflaged their factory in a wavy four-colour camouflage scheme, and the Hawker assembly shed, an easier building to conceal, had been cleverly repainted to resemble a row of houses, to blend in with those in nearby Byfleet. To add to the illusion false roads had been painted on the Byfleet Banking surface, with a real one cut through it to serve the Flying Village. Camouflage netting covered part of the Members' Banking area at the northern end of the airfield, mounted on wooden poles driven into the

'Wellington'
"BRISTOL" PEGASUS ENGINES
J. MAKOWSKY

concrete. In places it was so high that cars could be parked beneath it.

At the side of St. George's Hill, just across the road that ran past the Vickers main gate, was the Sandpits area. Here Vickers had built a network of underground shelters. Chicken wire had been stretched down the hill from the golf course above, metal swarf from the Vickers machine shop had been worked into it and the result sprayed dark green, so concealing the distinctive sandy bank. This area also included a first-aid centre, which was built in the style of a semi-sunk air-raid shelter, earth being heaped on top both for protection and camouflage. Installed within the factory were several conical concrete one-man shelters, surrounded by sandbags and intended for firewatchers. Semi-sunk shelters had also been provided near the Hawker shed. All these measures exceeded the standards laid down for the protection of the aircraft workers, and as events would show, they would become all too necessary.

Something that could not be concealed was the four-track London-Portsmouth main railway line, which ran along the northwest side of the airfield. This was also true of the distinctive triangular junction that connected a branch line to Addlestone and Staines. Several German pilots and racing drivers had visited Brooklands in pre-war days, and the skies above it had once played host to the German airship *Graf Zeppelin*, which had dipped its nose in salute as it cruised overhead after a race meeting in 1932. Could those pilots now find their way back under such very different circumstances?

Certainly the Germans were well aware of what was going on at Vickers. Six months before the outbreak of war the *Luftwaffe* had compiled an intelligence sheet on the factory and allocated the target number GB 747 to it. The airfield was called GB 1028.

The Hawker shed, which had originally witnessed the assembly of Hart and Osprey biplanes, was now fully engaged in the supply, repair and cannibalisation of shot-down Hurricanes. This latter process was applied to crashed or shot-down aircraft, and was an unpleasant job due to the reek of glycol and aviation spirit that often accompanied these wrecks.

The crack Erprobungsgruppe 210, equipped with both Bf110 and Bf109 fighter-bombers, had earned a reputation for both accuracy and courage in its attacks during August. To them was given the task of destroying the Vickers factory at Brooklands on 4th September. Here, one of the unit's Bf110s undergoes routine maintenance. (J. Vasco)

Vickers concentrated on the manufacture of Wellingtons and spare parts for those already on the bomber squadrons, while also providing some Spitfire undercarriage parts and modifications. During August, one visitor who would soon become famous had his Spitfire fitted with a camera-gun at the works. He was Flight Lieutenant Robert Stanford-Tuck, then serving with 92 Squadron in South Wales. The following day Tuck, while visiting Northolt, took off on his own to intercept a raid and was shot down, but baled out - one of many narrow escapes during his flying career.

Fresh and new in their green and brown war paint, Wellingtons stood waiting on the airfield for ferry pilots to collect them. Production carried on around the clock and development also continued with the Wellington's bigger brother, the Warwick, whose prototypes were now being tested with a variety of engines.

The Bofors tower on Members' Hill, and a large sandbagged observation post on top of the Sandpits, provided some means of visual warning, but the *Luftwaffe* attacks on RAF bases, and the damage done to them, showed quite clearly that any raid would be heavy and any warning of it would be brief. It would ultimately depend on the 'Mark 1 Human Eyeball' - on the alertness of the spotters and the efficiency of the warning system.

While the RDF chain covered the entire south coast, the equipment then in use was crude by modern standards. Due to difficulties in establishing whether an aircraft was in front of a station or behind it, the sets had been 'screened' so that they could only plot out to sea. They could cover the Channel and watch German bomber formations forming over France, but once these formations crossed the British coast Fighter Command was entirely dependent upon the Observer Corps to report their height, speed and course. This change in technique was described by Churchill as a reversion to the Stone Age, but these were desperate times and there was nothing else available. Observer Corps plots often proved a useful and timely source of information, but no system could ever be infallible. A great deal also depended on the weather, particularly when trying to track a formation at high altitude, and the skill of the Observer Corps in passing on details of an incoming raid from one post to another.

A degree of risk therefore had to be accepted by the aircraft factories, and by anyone else likely to become a target - which was just about all of Britain at this time. Fred Bint, a Hawker apprentice, remembered,

> "During that period we'd agreed to accept one-minute warnings, in order to have the minimum interference with aircraft production. The one-minute warning was effected by a large klaxon horn blower outside the Time Office, which was just inside the main entrance to the assembly shed."

At the Vickers factory a siren was mounted on the roof and from 1939 a system of colour-coded warnings had been in force. A single word, passed by telephone, could act as a preliminary warning, as a warning at night to extinguish all lighting exempt from blackout regulations, or as an all-clear.[1]

1. See Appendix I

A Bf110 of Erp.Gr.210 being loaded with a 250-kg bomb. (J. Vasco)

The first day of Göring's new strategy began with a series of airfield attacks. In the morning the RAF bases at Lympne and Eastchurch were raided, as was Bradwell-on-Sea in Essex. Shortly after lunchtime a second raid developed, and on RDF screens along the south coast many plots began to appear, stretching from Kent to Sussex. The Short Brothers factory at Rochester, producing Stirling bombers, was hit, as was the nearby Pobjoy aero-engine works. Some two hundred enemy aircraft were now approaching the coast on a broad front, saturating Fighter Command's plotting tables and stretching the depleted defences to the limit.

At 13.05 hours nine Hurricanes of 43 Squadron under Squadron Leader Caesar Hull were scrambled from RAF Tangmere in Sussex, quickly followed at 13.12 hours by eight Hurricanes of 601 (County of Middlesex) Squadron under Flight Lieutenant William Rhodes-Moorhouse. Churchill's much-quoted comment about 'the Few' was now more appropriate than he could have imagined, for each of these squadrons should have had at least twelve serviceable aircraft, with another six in reserve. Casualties in both men and machines had been heavy in the past few weeks, with the RAF at times losing more fighters than the *Luftwaffe*. While the factories were busy turning out new and repaired aircraft, a serious shortage of fully-trained pilots was beginning to make itself felt. Of those available, many had to go into action with less than the minimum number of hours 'on type' - meaning the type of fighter they would fly in - often against German veterans with experience dating back to the Spanish Civil War. Some British fighter pilots survived to learn the hard way, but many did not.

Based in No.10 Group's quieter sector at Middle Wallop in Hampshire, 234 Squadron, flying Spitfires under Flight Lieutenant Pat Hughes, was up to strength with twelve aircraft. In response to No.11 Group's call, 234 originally patrolled over Tangmere at 15,000 feet, just in case other raiders attempted to take advantage of the absence of 43 and 601 Squadrons.

The battle started at 13.20 hours, when all three squadrons sighted the enemy. The picture was confused, and with hindsight it appears that most of these aircraft were acting as a covering force to await the return of a separate raiding party. Hull and Rhodes-Moorhouse both saw many Messerschmitt 110s heading south from inland, while Hughes saw two enemy units. One was a group of Bf110s in a defensive circle in the Midhurst-Haslemere area, while another fifty '110s were approaching the coast from the Channel. All three squadrons attacked and a series of individual dogfights took place along the coast from Brighton to Littlehampton.

Among the raiders was a small but significant group of fourteen Bf110s from *Erprobungsgruppe 210*, led by *Hauptmann* von Boltenstern. This experimental unit had been formed to evaluate the Bf 109 and Bf 110 fighters in a fighter-bomber role. Two versions of the Bf 110, the C4/B and the D/O sub-types, both able to carry two 500-Kilo bombs under their slim fuselages, had been made available. The D type could also be fitted with a large ventral fuel tank, which gave its nose a swollen appearance and sometimes caused it to be mistaken for the larger Do17Z. *Epr 210* also used the Bf 110C-6, which was fitted with a single 30mm cannon in a bulged housing under the nose. It is not certain whether any of this type were used on 4th September, but if so they might also have been confused with the Do17Z. This could account for the various types of German

Hauptmann Karl von Boltenstern, who led the attack on 4th September. He never reached the English coast, for his Bf110 crashed into the Channel while evading an attack by RAF fighters.
(J. Vasco)

bomber reported by RAF pilots and by other witnesses on the ground on that day.

Based at Denain in France, *Epr 210* had taken off at 06.30 hours that morning and flown to a forward base at Calais-Marck. Shortly after midday they took off again and headed across the Channel with an escort of other Bf110s from *V(Z)/LG 1*, an operational development unit made up of experienced crews and intended to test new tactics.

As they approached the Sussex coast the two units spotted the RAF fighters preparing to attack. Von Boltenstern's Bf110 dived in an attempt to avoid them and crashed into the Channel, killing him and his gunner, *Feldwebel* Schneider.

Designed as a twin-engined long-range fighter, the Bf110 had performed well in its early actions and those who flew it had been regarded by Göring as something of an elite. However, although fast, it was sluggish when taking evasive action and the single machine gun in its rear cockpit was hardly an adequate defence against the eight guns of the RAF fighters.

Engines whined, guns stuttered and one by one black streaks appeared in the sky as '110s began to fall.

Despite the loss of von Boltenstern, his crews were determined to destroy one source of the RAF's supply of new aircraft, be they fighters or bombers. Their target was the Vickers factory at Brooklands.[2]

Thomas Barrett was a gunner with 301 Battery of the 98th Heavy Anti-Aircraft Regiment at the Woburn Park site.

> "We were out in a field at Addlestone. The gun sites had no concrete or sandbags then - they were just out in the open. We'd dug holes for air-raid shelters, and our toilet consisted of a trench with a pole across it! Captain Edwards, the battery commander, was a good officer and provided the detachments did their duties in the morning they could generally have the afternoons to themselves. There were some people on duty, but I was on the grass sunbathing at the time."

The other Bf110 units had successfully served as a diversion, drawing off the three defending squadrons they had met at the coast. Now *Epr 210* were behind the RDF screen and no-one but the Observer Corps could track their progress. Still with their escort, they flew a complicated series of feints and their track was lost in the Horsham area, merging, as far as the 11 Group controllers could see, into the general battle. It was a bright, warm summer's day, cloudless but with some haze, making ground observation of aircraft at altitude difficult and their identification even more so.

Despite the indifferent quality of some of their aircraft, *Epr 210* were building up a reputation as a crack unit. By the end of 1940 they would have several successful fighter-bomber attacks to their credit. Not that things had always gone smoothly. On 15th August a navigation error had led them to bomb Croydon Airport instead of RAF Kenley, although in so doing they had hit what had now become a fighter base. Some bombs had fallen on the nearby Rollason aircraft works, at which Hurricanes had been repaired and where Wellingtons were fitted with anti-magnetic mine hoops after the initial trials work had been carried out at Weybridge. Specially formed for attacks on Britain, *Epr 210's* badge was a red map of the British Isles with

---

2. A surviving *Epr 210* pilot's logbook clearly states, 'Vickers, Brooklands,' not the Hawker shed, which has frequently been claimed as the target on that day.

A camera-gun mounted on a British fighter records the destruction of a Bf110 during the Battle of Britain. The streaky trails on the right are caused by tracer bullets. (IWM C2433)

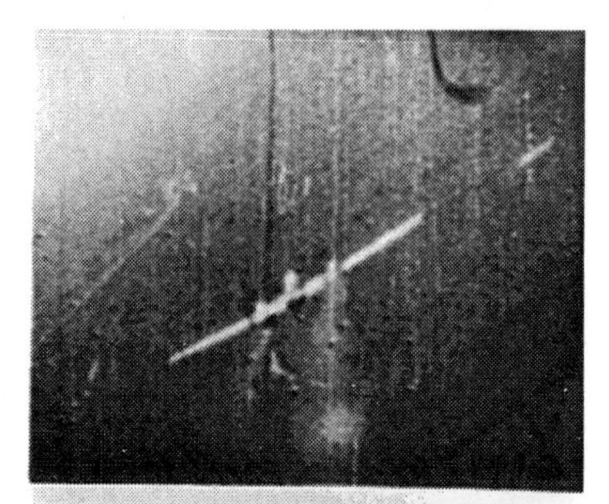

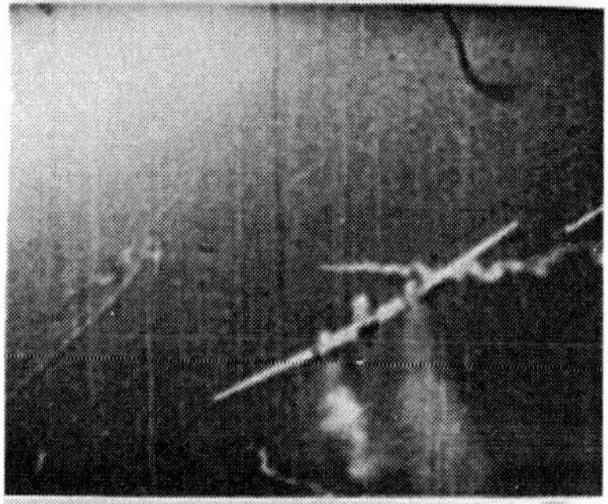

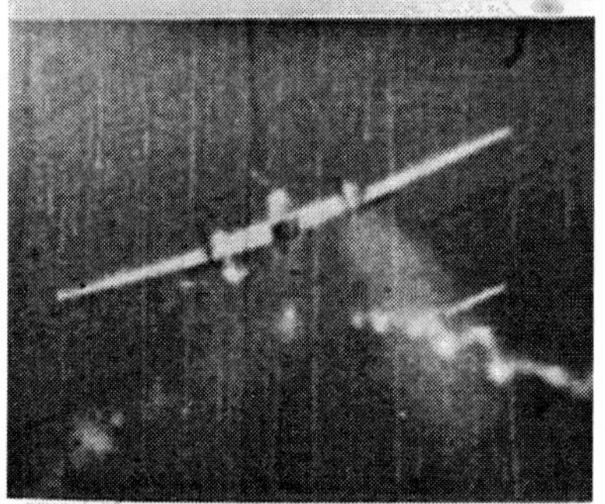

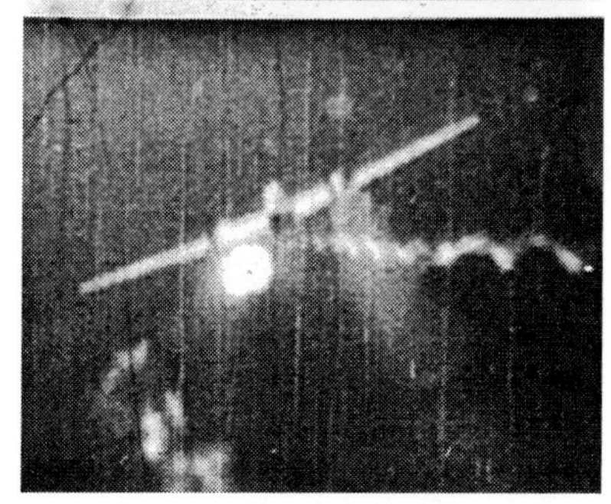

a yellow gunsight superimposed on it.

The exact route of this unit and its escort is not entirely clear, nor is the motive for the two separate groups of Bf110s seen flying across Brooklands from different directions simultaneously. What seems probable is that the escort, flying above, up-sun and to one side of their charges, flew past the airfield and then turned back, to fly over *Epr 210* and defend them from the fighter attack that followed. What is clear, from the testimony of witnesses on the ground and surviving records, is that one group of 110s flew up from the Cobham area, to the south of their target. A second group, 'flying by Bradshaw' along the railway line, turned back from the Walton area to approach Brooklands from the northwest.

At the Vickers factory all was normal, for no alarm had yet been sounded. The lunchtime period was about to end and a queue of workers was forming at the time clock in the passageway between the machine and erecting shops to register for the afternoon shift. Having clocked on early, some went back outside to enjoy the sun for a few more minutes. Ernest Babb, a fitter, had gone home to Ashford for lunch, calling in at a small Post Office-cum-store by the main gate for a cup of tea before returning to work. The sound of approaching aircraft caused no comment at the time, for such sounds were commonplace at a factory airfield.

The escorting Bf110s were seen by an Observer Corps post near Guildford as they headed northeast, reaching their target at 13.24 hours. Still there was no siren, although at the last moment the heavy guns opened fire. Gunner Barrett's sunbathing came to an abrupt end.

> "They dived out of the sun. I got to the gun very quickly, and as it was my job to regulate the shell fuses by means of a dial I didn't see the action directly. I'm convinced we blew one out of the sky, though. I can remember the others cheering. I think what gave the game away was the Vickers staff sunbathing in white coats during lunchtime. The factory was pleased with us though - they had a collection for us afterwards."

The first alarm was sounded by a man clocking on at the Hawker shed. He saw the Bf110s diving out of the sun and slammed his hand onto a nearby klaxon as the bombs began to fall, but it was too late now. As though chained together a pair of bombs plunged towards the Vickers works. Others followed as one aircraft strafed the ground, sending a line of spurts zigzagging across the concrete. One bomb landed at the Fork, damaging the grandstand that still stood there. Another fell in a nearby repair hangar and a third scored a direct hit on a shelter in which some factory girls were eating their lunch.

However, it was the one that fell through the factory roof that did the most damage. Crashing down through the stairwell leading from the first-floor canteen, it landed on top of a heavy press in the machine shop and exploded close to the time clock, killing many queueing workers. Hearing the first bombs whistle down, Ernest Babb dived beneath the store's table and stayed there as bottles fell from the shelves to clatter around him.

In anticipation of the raids, the Vickers Drawing Office had already been moved to the golf clubhouse at Burhill, a few miles away. Norman 'Spud' Boorer, caught in the middle of lunchtime

THE AEROPLANE
DEC. 20, 1940
Walton
high speed craft for
air co-operation
Fast tenders for service, repair and rescue work
Medium Speed general utility launches
THE WALTON YACHT WORKS LTD.

revolver practice with the Home Guard, was glad of that move as he watched the diving '110s attack. Even so, some of his colleagues had narrow escapes. David James, a stressman, had been driving with a friend to Burhill as the '110s passed above. Reaching the junction of the Brooklands and Byfleet Roads, they hurriedly leapt into the gutter as several bombs fell short, exploding on St. George's Hill. Still under his table, Ernest Babb heard a voice shouting, 'Get out of there!' and quickly did so. 'The sunny day saved my life,' he later recalled. 'If the weather had been bad I'd have gone back into the factory early.' Others would owe their lives to that same decision.

The Bofors detachments around the airfield quickly came to life, but did not fire a shot, as by the time they were ready their intended targets had gone. The Parachute-and-Cable detachment did not fire their rockets either, as none of the raiders came low enough. The attack was all over in three minutes.

The heavy guns claimed two aircraft destroyed. Word of the impending raid had not reached the light guns in time, but even if it had it would have been difficult to fight off what seemed to be two simultaneous attacks from different directions. Now it was time for the escort to prove their worth, for as it turned out, not every RAF fighter had been drawn into the south coast battle.

Nine Hurricanes of 253 Squadron, under Flight Lieutenant William Cambridge, had been ordered up from Kenley in Surrey to patrol between there and Croydon. Cambridge had been given a series of contradictory plots by the Kenley controller, with enemy aircraft reported as coming in from the southeast, the southwest and finally the west, which showed the confusion reigning in the No.11 Group Operations Room at this time. He had been told to climb to 8,000 feet, but knowing from recent bitter experience that height was what counted, he steadily led his men to 12,000, keeping into the sun and determined to get above any opposition that might be sighted. It was then that he spotted *Epr 210*, just as they were about to bomb.

Although Cambridge misidentified the aircraft as 'Jaguars' - a propaganda nickname and also one applied to the Messerschmitt Bf163 prototype - which in fact saw no action - there could be no doubt as to their nationality or their intended purpose.

The Hurricanes wheeled to starboard in 'vic' formation and dived out of the sun.

At 6,000 feet the two sides met. Cambridge picked a target, and as he expended all his ammunition in one long burst the German's port engine caught fire. Opposing fire from the rear gunner was quickly silenced and the '110 stall-turned to port. Still firing, Cambridge dived after it, seeing it crash in flames near a farm some six miles from Brooklands. His fellow flight commander, Flight Lieutenant J H Wedgewood, got onto the tail of a '110 and fired a ten-second burst, closing from 250 yards to point-blank range. The '110 caught fire, climbed steeply for a second and then fell, crashing into a wood. A '110 dived with an apparent cockpit fire after an attack by Pilot Officer W M C Samolinski, as did one that was shot up at close quarters by Sergeant A S Dredge. Smoke burst from the fuselage of a '110 attacked by Pilot Officer T Nowak, Pilot Officer A H Corkett's victim came down in a field and Sergeant E H C Kee damaged another in a head-on attack. Sergeant R A Innes and Flying Officer R D H Watts both claimed to have silenced the rear gunners of two Bf110s.

Curiously, despite the claims of the heavy gunners below, who in their own report credited the Hurricanes with one kill, none of the surviving pilots' combat report forms mentions any anti-aircraft bursts, or admits to seeing any enemy aircraft shot down in this manner. However, it should be appreciated that in the kaleidoscopic whirl of a dogfight not even the most vigilant of fighter pilots could expect to see all of what happened.

All nine Hurricane pilots attacked without loss to themselves, and six 110s were claimed shot down by them. 253 Squadron returned to Kenley, no doubt satisfied, but unaware that it had been the escort that they had attacked. Again *Epr 210* had taken full advantage of the confusion and had headed for home at full speed. Luck had been with them - apart from von Boltenstern's accidental crash they had suffered no losses that day. Post-war research has shown that *V(Z)/LG 1* lost only four aircraft, so 253's claims were optimistic, and it is certainly possible that more than one Hurricane fired at the same Bf110. Only two aircraft were actually brought down by the 253 Squadron pilots. One aircraft crashed near Waterloo Farm, at the village of West Horsley - this was probably the one claimed by Cambridge. Its wounded gunner, *Unteroffizier* J Jäckel, bailed out and was taken prisoner, but his pilot, *Feldwebel* Karl Röhring, was killed. A second '110 came down on Netley Common, near Dorking. From this one there were no survivors.

Black smoke poured from the Vickers factory and chaos reigned on the airfield. A frantic 'phone call to the Hawker shed had resulted in that firm's first aiders leaping into the first available vehicle and heading across towards the works. Just as they reached a bridge crossing the Wey the sirens sounded. Everyone leapt out of the vehicle and threw themselves down on the river bank, expecting a second attack. It was some minutes before they realized that this was the alarm that should have preceded the first one!

Hawker and Vickers staff, aided by soldiers from a Royal Artillery searchlight battery who had been acting as airfield guards, spent a gruesome afternoon removing both dead and wounded from within the factory. A fire was extinguished by the AFS, leaving a pall of smoke and brick dust hanging over the area. 20th Guards Brigade, whose headquarters was nearby on St. George's Hill, sent fifty men over for a task laconically described in their War Diary as 'clearing wreckage, etc.'

Casualties were brought across Brooklands Road to the Sandpits area for treatment. An assortment of vehicles, including Home Guard armoured cars, used both lanes of the road in removing them from there to hospital. Despite the pressure, local doctors were agreeably surprised at the standard of first aid given. However, for all too many of those brought out there was only one course of action. The local mortuary was unable to cope with all the dead, and Mount Felix Hall in Weybridge was temporarily pressed into use. Four bodies were never identified, and of the girls in the shelter little was ever found. The toll had been a heavy one, with 83 dead and 419 wounded.[3] It would have been worse had the staff still been working the seven-day week that had been instituted at the outbreak of war. Unable to maintain that level of effort indefinitely, by mid-1940 they had gone onto an eight-day rota, and consequently many were absent when the raid occurred. It would also have been far more damaging if the Germans had bombed Vickers ten minutes later, for by then the factory would have been fully manned and the carnage within it much higher.

Dick Lewis, then a schoolboy, had come home for lunch at his father's motorcycle shop in Weybridge. It was about to be served when the first bomb landed. 'It was mince, which I didn't like then or now. I can never see it without thinking of what happened that day.' Later in the afternoon he watched as dishevelled groups of workers made their way home into Weybridge along Heath Road. Some were walking, others were pushing bicycles, and many were covered in brick dust. Shock took many forms, from the irate elderly warden who danced up and down after it was all over, shouting, 'They never got me in the last war and they'll never get me in this!' to a repeat, a year later almost to the day, of the same heavy dullness that Peggy Millson had noticed. The unthinkable had finally happened, and Weybridge was now as much in the front line as any other British town.

George Roake was then a young panel beater in the Vickers tin shop, and had been one of the last to see the girls who died in the shelter.

---

3. See Appendix IV

> "The next day I got a sort of repercussion of what had happened, and I said, 'I've got to go back - they don't know whether I'm dead or not.' So I went back and I met Mr Greenwood, who was the foreman, and gave him my name. He said, 'Well, lad, you can come back and start if you like. We've got no roof on!' I went back up to the tin shop. We were working with pieces of wood and tarpaulins over our benches, and no roof on at all. You could look up and see an aeroplane fly by!"

Fortunately most of the traffic overhead was friendly, as fighter patrol activity over Brooklands was stepped up. Again, aircraft from both Nos.10 and 11 Groups took part. Some Vickers departments closed down temporarily while arrangements were made to disperse component production into the surrounding area. Although serious, the raid had not been as devastating as the Germans would have liked. The Hawker shed had not yet been touched and the production of Hurricanes continued. Having experienced several previous false alerts, the Vickers staff had at one time treated air-raid warnings as something of a joke. Now they became almost too sensitive. Morale at the factory slumped, and those who came back to work were jittery for a long time afterwards. Bill Vincent, an electrician who had been in the factory and dived between two roof stanchions to save himself, said later, 'I wasn't hurt, but I tell you, I had the runs when any alert sounded after that!'

When an alert occurred, some people ran madly out of the factory and across Brooklands Road for the shelters, regardless of whether they collided with vehicles or each other on the way. Some tripped coming down the stairs and were kicked or trodden on by others behind them. Had the Germans maintained the pressure by a series of raids neither Vickers nor the Hawker shed would have been able to keep production going for long - and the target date for invasion was no more than a couple of weeks away.

The factory would be rebuilt, although in the building and in the minds of those who had been there the effects would linger on for decades to come. Holes punched by flying shrapnel remained visible in several girders used as roof supports in the corridor between the machine and erecting shops. They would stay there until the factory was finally demolished in the spring of 1990. Two pieces of damaged girder and the roof siren have since been acquired by Brooklands Museum for display.

As already noted, Ernest Babb survived the bombing with not so much as a scratch, but three months later he developed a rash. This was first thought to be industrial dermatitis, but was later diagnosed to be the result of a delayed nervous reaction. When he was interviewed for this book nearly fifty years later, he was still occasionally suffering from it.

Chapter Five

Second Chance

As Vickers set about picking up the pieces the battle overhead continued. Although the gun defences were part of the British Army's Anti-Aircraft Command, that formation in turn was subject to the orders of Fighter Command. Because of the Brooklands raid a new standing order improving the manning of light AA guns was quickly issued. From now on, half the detachments would 'stand-to' by their weapons at all times. The remainder, although engaged on other duties, would of course 'stand-to' if an alert occurred.

The night of 5/6th September 1940 was a quiet one in Surrey, apart from a few bombs dropped on Oxshott Common shortly after midnight. On the following morning the appearance of many reconnaissance aircraft suggested a return to bombing of the aircraft factories. In response to Park's request Brand sent Spitfires of 609 Squadron over from No.10 Group to protect Brooklands. It was becoming familiar territory for them; they had patrolled over there on the afternoon of the 4th after being scrambled too late to catch those responsible for the raid. On this day they would again miss the action; for the second time in two days it would be the Hurricane that would be called upon to defend its birthplace.

Between 08.36 and 08.58 hours six separate raids were plotted over Kent. After crossing the coast they fanned out into four groups over the Maidstone area, with roughly three fighters to each bomber. One group headed towards Chatham, a second towards the RAF fighter bases at Hornchurch and North Weald, a third towards Tunbridge Wells and the fourth towards the Kenley-Biggin Hill area.

At 08.45 hours eight Hurricanes of 1 Squadron left Northolt with orders to join 303 (Polish) Squadron and patrol over Kenley at 20,000 feet. Two other Hurricanes later took off from Northolt at 09.20 hours to join them. Flight Lieutenant M H

Brooklands-built Hurricane P3395 of No.1 Squadron, pictured here at Wittering in October 1940, took part in the second heavy daylight raid over Brooklands on 6th September 1940. The pilot is Sergeant Arthur Clowes, a veteran of the Battle of France. Clowes was unsuccessful on 6th September, but was credited with the destruction of a Bf110 over the Thames estuary next day. (IWM CH17331)

Brown, leading the squadron, did not meet up with his Polish colleagues and was going east on the edge of the patrol area when he saw a formation of German fighters on his right and above. He then sighted a very large formation of bombers on his left, stepped up backwards in 'vics' of three and five aircraft. All were going west, the fighters at some distance from their charges and up-sun of them.

Brown had not been informed of the presence of this formation and, as their escort were above him, he was not in a favourable position. However he ordered the squadron into line astern and turned left to attack the bombers. Chasing a Ju88 that crossed under him, Brown fired a five-second burst, then broke away to avoid collision, having silenced the rear gunner and hit the starboard engine. He did not see his victim again.

Among the Bf110s identified in this formation were, once again, *Epr 210* and *V(Z)/LG 1*. *I/ZG26* was also there, possibly as escort to the bomber unit *KG76*, whose target was Kenley. By accident or design *Epr 210* and their escort had become part of a bigger enterprise this time. Aware that their success two days before had been only a partial one - although doubtless some Vickers staff would not have agreed - they had returned to finish the job they had started.

Some eighty enemy aircraft were involved and for them the battle began in the Kenley-Tunbridge Wells area. The presence of some stragglers showed that this formation had been attacked before 1 Squadron had met it. Nevertheless the Germans pressed on, turning southwest, possibly as a feint towards the Hawker works at Kingston, then northwest towards Brooklands. An air battle was seen over the Walton area as 1 Squadron pressed home their attack. Empty cartridge cases and belt links clattered onto the streets below, to be gathered up as souvenirs by local children. Some enemy aircraft jettisoned their loads at Ewell and Leatherhead, but no bombs fell on Kenley.

At 09.11 hours the sirens wailed over Weybridge and the aircraft workers hurriedly made for the shelters. One minute later the first bombs began to fall on the airfield. They were seen by Pilot Officer R H Dibnah of 1 Squadron, who had turned back early with propeller trouble and had been returning to Northolt. Despite his problem Dibnah carried out a quarter attack on the Bf110 formation, which was estimated by him to be between seventy and eighty enemy aircraft. Other Hurricanes followed and the enemy turned back towards the coast. Dibnah followed, and near Redhill he saw a Bf110 break away from the formation to engage two Hurricanes. As they broke away Dibnah attacked this aircraft from the beam, causing it to stall-turn. Each then flew at the other head-on, and the '110 turned as it roared past him. By now his fire had evidently taken effect, for his target spiralled down and hit the ground at Crowhurst, near Oxted in Surrey. The pilot, *Unteroffizier* Gerhard Rüger, was killed, although his gunner, *Gefreiter* Edmund Ernst, baled out and was taken prisoner.

Epr 210 had lost another Bf110 for no real gain, as aircraft production at Brooklands was not halted for long. This time no bombs hit the Vickers factory. However, ten landed on the airfield, two of which fell on the tarmac by the Hawker shed and

Bf110s of Erprobungsgruppe 210 in flight. S9+BH, in the right background, was flown by Unteroffizier Gerhard Rüger when it was shot down after the second Brooklands attack on 6th September.
(J. Vasco).

caused some damage to it. Hurricane production stopped for the day due to the presence of one unexploded bomb.[4]

There were two minor casualties among the Hawker staff. One was James Lomas, who had been working at the Hawker flight shed in the Flying Village, and also on the cannibalisation of crashed fighters that had been returned to the assembly shed. Classified as an 'improver', which surprised him as he had not gone through the apprenticeship previously deemed necessary for such a trade, he was also a Hawker Home Guard member.

> "I was practising on a small range on a bit of spare ground behind Thomson and Taylors, the car designers. When the alert sounded I sprinted from there to a Lewis gun pit with Ray Smithers, a colleague."

The Lewis, a drum-fed First World War relic whose complicated mechanism frequently led to stoppages, was widely used in 1940 for airfield defence, not because it was ideal but because there was nothing else to be had.

> "I'd fired off half a drum of ammunition when the gun jammed and a bomb landed close to the pit. I saw the sandbags bulge in towards me, then out and back into place again! I didn't realise I'd been hit until I saw blood on the pit floor. They rushed me to hospital in a Beaverette armoured car

---

4. There is no record of this bomb having been found. It may have been treated as a false alarm, and then been the one found in that area in 1990!

driven by Les Wilson, a pre-war Thomson and Taylor mechanic. It was a pretty hairy ride! I got ten stitches in my arm - I think it was a lump of shrapnel."

ZG26 lost two Bf110s to fighter action. Brown's Ju88, which had also been attacked by his colleague Pilot Officer C M Stavert, dumped its bombs and crash-landed near Tonbridge. All four crew members survived. It was one of the two aircraft from *6/KG76* lost on this date. The Bofors gunners at Brooklands also claimed one bomber shot down at Ottershaw Park, to the west of the airfield.

In contrast to the Vickers raid of two days before, this raid had some amusing aspects, rather than tragic ones. A collection of vintage cars and aircraft had been assembled by R G J 'Dick' Nash, a Brooklands racing driver, in the interwar period and hired out by him for film work, sometimes on the racetrack and airfield, which had played host to actors as diverse as George Formby, Will Hay and Laurence Olivier. These items had been kept by him in a shed at the Flying Village, next to Thomson and Taylors, who had designed, built and tuned many famous cars, including Sir Malcolm Campbell's Bluebird. Sadly, one bomb made a direct hit on Nash's shed, leaving nothing but a large crater, and scattering the contents in all directions. R L Beauchamp, a draughtsman at Thomson and Taylors, came back to his drawing office, in an ex-RFC building known as the Hermitage, to find an old Mercedes car, dating from the turn of the century, embedded in its roof! Hawkers had their problems too - a Model T Ford had been blown through the roof of a recently-erected Bellman hangar and had come to rest suspended by its front axle from a girder, hanging just above a parked Hurricane. The fighter, which was undamaged, was moved out and the car was then allowed to drop.

Nash's loss was a substantial one, although fortunately his shed had been taken over by Brooklands Aviation, another firm at the Flying Village, earlier that summer, and some items had been moved out before the bombing. He was unable to understand why the *Luftwaffe* had apparently singled him out, and later commented to Beauchamp that his shed had been the most unmilitary building on the site!

Unteroffizier Gerhard Rüger was killed in action on 6th September 1940, shot down after bombing Brooklands. He is pictured here as a Flieger (Airman) (J.Vasco)

With invasion now thought to be only a matter of days away, and Brooklands a possible target for German airborne troops, a more serious loss had been caused by a hit on the ERA Company's sheds, which had housed the armoury of the Hawker Home Guard contingent. A W 'Boyd' Kelly, a Hawker ground engineer and Home Guard member, recalled that

> "We had about a dozen men armed with Canadian 0.303 Ross rifles. We lost most of these weapons in this raid, as well as tin hats. They got blown everywhere, including the sewage farm!"

This foul-smelling area, which had been made up from land given by Hugh Locke King to Woking Borough Council in the 1890s, before he had seen the need for a racetrack, was located between the Flying Village hangars and the track's Railway Straight. Several pilots had 'ditched' in it during the pioneering days of aviation and it had become part of the Brooklands legend. A more spectacular occurrence than the flight of the rifles was the bronze machine gun mounting that was blown over the banking and through the roof of a house in Byfleet, half a mile away.

This day was Ted Petty's 21st birthday, and it was one coming-of-age that he would never forget. After seeing the Hawker armoury go up, two Vickers armoured cars crossed the airfield to see what assistance they could give. Ted found a Ross rifle bayonet, the pommel of which had been scraped where it had hit the concrete, and kept it as a souvenir.

> "At the back of the Flying Village was a line of sheds and other buildings. I don't know who the people were who lived in them. One of these had been hit and the blast was such that it left it almost intact, but lying on its side. I remember walking on what had been a wall, trying not to tread on the pictures! At the back there was an Anderson shelter, and we saw this dear old lady come out of it. She was all right, though. She took one look at the wreckage and her first words were, 'Oh, what a bloody mess!"

The intervention of 1 Squadron had made little difference to *Epr 210's* attack, but they did not return to Brooklands again. Despite their skill in the pioneering of fighter-bomber techniques, their fortunes would eventually fade with those of the rest of the *Luftwaffe*. However the unit later mounted further attacks on the Supermarine works at Southampton and the Parnall Aircraft factory at Yate, near Bristol, with mixed results. After their inability to defend the airfield two days before, the Bofors gunners must have celebrated this time and, before the day was out, a new element would be added to the Brooklands defences.

RAF Balloon Command, whose No.30 Group covered much of southeastern England, was also responsible to Fighter Command for defence, its units being organized in squadrons. Given the low-level nature of the attack on the 4th and the possibility of a repetition, some kind of deterrent was needed to inhibit low flying - and what better obstacle than a barrage balloon?

A quick-response unit, 992 Rover Squadron, arrived at Brooklands that evening and became operational at 22.00 hours. Veterans of a string of sites from Dorset to Dover, this unit was made up of assorted flights and members of 902, 903 and 904 Squadrons, becoming formalized as 954 Squadron on the 18th. By day a 'lane' would be left through the Brooklands balloon barrage for visiting friendly aircraft, but it would be closed at night, when, weather permitting, all twenty-four balloons, in three flights of eight, would be up.

The deterrent value of the barrage was illustrated within days by the pilot of a Bristol Blenheim. Intending to land, he took one look at the gleaming silver monsters now dotted round the airfield and quickly changed his mind! The whole Weybridge area was becoming a place for aircraft of both sides to avoid, as events were soon to prove.

Many units of the Canadian Army had come to Britain during 1940, and had been posted to Surrey. Among them was the West Nova Scotia Regiment, which had been under canvas in a field near East Horsley since July. Although they had witnessed many day and night raids, so far their only taste of action had been the capture of a wounded *Luftwaffe* airman on 15th August. After bandaging his wounds and offering him a cigarette, they had taken him under guard to their Divisional headquarters, and in good bureaucratic fashion had obtained a receipt! On 4th September they had provided a crash guard for an enemy aircraft shot down by 253 Squadron near the village of Shere. On the 6th their diarist commented,

> "The air of tension and expectancy is more pronounced today, and everybody went about their tasks with the feeling that something was about to happen."

That something was the threatened invasion. On the evening of the 4th Hitler had made a surprise appearance at a Nazi Party rally in Berlin, declaring that if the RAF dared to continue their attacks on German cities, British ones would be wiped out. So when would the invasion begin? 'In England they ask, 'Why isn't he coming?' Be patient. He's coming! He's coming!'

Like everyone else in Britain the Canadians expected warning of the invasion any time now. They would not have much longer to wait.

Chapter Six
Danger UXB

On the afternoon of 7th September 1940 *Reichsmarschall* Hermann Göring, resplendent in a gold-braided sky-blue uniform, stood on the cliffs near Calais and watched as the *Luftwaffe* roared overhead in several massive waves. There were nearly one thousand aircraft, stacked up from 14,000 to 23,000 feet, occupying some eight hundred square miles of sky and advancing on a twenty-mile front across the Thames estuary. It quickly became clear to Fighter Command controllers that this was the biggest raid they had yet faced. For this there could only be one target, and all the available squadrons in the south were ordered to London's defence, but they were not enough to stop the first deliberate raid on the capital in this war. The East End began to burn, and one shocked Canadian Army unit in Surrey noted in its War Diary that it was if the sky itself was on fire.

The diarist of the West Nova Scotia Regiment wrote that on the night of the 7th the anti-aircraft fire lasted from dusk until dawn the next day, and that although two bombs screamed down to land over a mile away, they felt much closer.

> "The nightly coterie of stargazers around Battalion HQ did some ducking for cover. The sandbagged AA pit across the road was filled to overflowing with men piled in any old way on top of one another. These are the lads who've been craving action. The AA gunners were heard to remark that they guessed they'd have lots of help enlarging the pit tomorrow."

Despite this, there would be even more night watchers in the future, for the continuing tension was making sleep hard to come by.

Air Vice Marshal Park and his AOC, Air Chief Marshal Sir Hugh Dowding, viewed the heavy damage and civilian casualties with mixed feelings. Both could be forgiven for feeling relieved, for Göring's change of target had given Fighter

On 7th September, the weight of the Luftwaffe fell upon london. A bomber stream some twenty miles wide and fifty miles long headed for the capital. He111s, like these depicted, formed a large part of the attack. With the coming of night, they came again. (IWM GER530)

Command the breathing space that it had been denied over the past few weeks. Now there would be time to patch up the fighter airfields and get the bombed aircraft factories working again.

The *Luftwaffe* attacks continued throughout the night of the 7th, guided by the huge conflagration they had started in London's docklands that afternoon, but, as the Canadians had noted, some bombs were still scattered. At 21.20 hours five fell on open ground in the Molesey Road area east of Walton, with another three close by. There was no damage or any casualties, although several residents of St. George's Hill reported whistling unexploded bombs falling. Nothing was found and these were thought to have been AA shell nose-caps returning to earth.

During the night many red flares were dropped by the bombers and sixteen incendiaries fell near the Fairmile Common gun site, being extinguished by the fire picket. An invasion alert was declared, with the code word *Parasols*, suggesting a parachute landing, being passed by the Army's Aldershot Command to the Woking Home Guard. Church bells rang throughout that district - the agreed invasion signal - and all over southern England men turned out to repel the first possible invasion since the Norman Conquest. However, it turned out to be a false alarm. The real invasion, codenamed *Operation Sea Lion*, was scheduled for 21st September 1940.

9th September 1940

At 03.45 hours a single enemy aircraft circled Brooklands, then dropped a stick of four bombs and two incendiaries. The first fell some thirty yards from the Hawker shed and the rest across the sewage farm, the last landing on the down local railway line and holding up rail traffic for over five hours. At 04.30 hours two large and four small bombs fell on Council land in the Weybridge district, accompanied by two oil bombs. Little damage and no casualties resulted from these two incidents.

Another return to aircraft factory targets was suggested by a large force of enemy aircraft seen late in the afternoon to the southwest of Brooklands. 253 Squadron, which had taken off from Kenley to patrol between there and Biggin Hill, met

While the Battle of Britain was reaching its climax, some of the victims of the Vickers raid were buried at Burvale cemetery, 9th September 1940. (Elmbridge Museum, 152. Frame 174 1964/4)

thirty-four Ju88s with escort at 15,000 feet. Anti-aircraft fire from the Wisley Common site burst in the centre of the bomber formation, which turned south while the Hurricanes were engaged by its escort. This time the dogfight was so confused that 253's pilots made no individual claims, but five Ju88s were claimed as probably destroyed by the squadron as a whole. This time none of the bombers reached Brooklands. It was not known until later that their intended target had been the London docks.

False alarms or not, the invasion threat remained, and the West Nova Scotia Regiment held a conference in their Orderly Room marquee that evening. Grim-faced men in battledress sat in the dimly-lit tent, burdened by tin hats and gas mask packs across their chests. The throbbing drone of enemy aircraft overhead, accompanied by a bomb falling in the distance, added to the sense of realism. 'At last we felt that our training days were at an end.' Afterwards the Canadians slept fitfully, convinced they would be in action before the morning.

Yet still there was no sign of a ground attack. Those Germans who had got home from the afternoon's dogfight over Surrey reported attacks by up to seventy RAF fighters and few people in Britain yet knew that the RAF's continuing resistance had caused a postponement of *Operation Sea Lion*.

10th September 1940

At 16.55 hours a Ju88 was seen at 5,000 feet, flying southwest. It was engaged by the heavy guns and chased by three Hurricanes. The result of this combat was not seen. Having seen the barrage balloons, the German had turned away before coming within range of the Bofors guns. Between 17.02-17.04 hours another lone Ju88 suddenly dived out of cloud over Brooklands and dropped eight bombs, none of which did any damage. It was unsuccessfully fired on by two heavy gun sites before climbing back into cloud again.

Five bombs and twelve one-Kilo incendiaries fell near Whiteley at 20.30 hours, the resulting fires being controlled by the AFS. Then, at 23.25, seven bombs, one carrying oil, fell near Albany Bridge and Molesey Road, leaving three double craters and slight property damage. Families in two houses had a curious escape, for their shelters were demolished but they survived, having remained in their homes this time! By now many people had come to the conclusion that taking refuge under the stairs was safer and more convenient than running outside to the shelter. Some, who had become too tired to care what happened, refused to rise at all, and on this occasion two children were lucky when a large block of earth dropped through a house roof onto their bed. There were no casualties.

12th September 1940

At 00.15 hours a 110-pound HE bomb fell fifty yards from a pair of isolated bungalows east of Seven Hills Road. There were no casualties.

18th September 1940

Following an alert at 20.04 hours, twelve bombs and fifty incendiaries fell, the latter mostly on open ground near the

The devastating effect of a 500-kg bomb that failed to explode. Dropped from around 12,000 feet, this bomb penetrated the roof, passed through the first floor and demolished the front wall before burying itself in the garden.

Burhill Road cemetery. Four of the bombs fell near the Terrace Road recreation ground and at least four others near Burhill golf course, with another landing in a garden in the Oatlands area of Weybridge. There was some property damage but no casualties.

So far the Weybridge district had got off fairly lightly, but other areas had suffered a good deal more, as was shown on the 19th when two hundred people from London's docklands were evacuated to this part of Surrey with just a day's warning. They were in a distressed state, and some had gone without a wash for the past two weeks. All were immediately given a free change of clothes by a clothing bureau that had opened at Mount Felix Hall in Weybridge. Local canteens provided a free meal on arrival and somehow everyone had been billeted by that evening. Evacuees were nothing new to this area - the Chief Billeting Officer noted that by now the district had accommodated a total of 492 people, over half from London.

21st September 1940

This Saturday morning dawned misty and quiet. It had been a week since that crucial and now famous air battle over southern England on the 15th, which had led Hitler, two days later, to again postpone *Operation Sea Lion*. He had intended that it should start on this day. However, on the British side of the Channel few were as yet aware that the invasion had been put off. Anyway, there were still other dangers. One of them arrived at Brooklands shortly after eight that morning.

After the Vickers bombing a company of the 1st Battalion of the Royal Canadian Engineers, based at Boxhill, near Dorking, had been given the job of removing broken glass from the erecting shop roof. Recently shipped to Britain and new to the war, they had remained at their work even after the alerts had sounded, and had become fond of shouting, 'You'll never win a war that way!' to the rapidly departing Vickers workers below them.

Thus far none of the Canadian troops in Britain had seen any action. As volunteers, they were clearly eager to prove themselves. Ted Petty remembered the Boxhill-based sappers as a fairly rough lot.

> "We used to play baseball with them on the track outside the Clubhouse during lunchtime. It stopped them from going down into Weybridge and causing havoc in the local pubs!"

On the 21st a section under the command of Lieutenant John Patton was working there.

A single Junkers 88 followed the railway line from Guildford and was seen over West Weybridge station just before 08.30 hours. Heading towards Walton, the German pilot skirted the balloon barrage, then on reaching Weybridge he swung round to starboard and dived down the 'lane' left open for landing aircraft. The heavy and light guns opened fire, some Bofors shells bursting just in front of the bomber's nose, but the Ju88 was a tough design and the crew of this one were evidently good at keeping their nerve. The bomber kept on course and released its load at low level, aiming at the Hawker shed. 'Boyd' Kelly, on Home Guard duty at the time, manned a Vickers gun in a weapon pit and fired back. The Ju88 roared over the banking

The Ju88 was fast, adaptable and solidly-built. It superseded the older He111 and was built in enormous numbers. Operating on every front, Ju88 crews could be tough and dangerous opponents.
(IWM MH6115)

and away, closely followed by a Hurricane pilot, Squadron Leader A D Murray of 501 Squadron from Kenley. He chased it south for several miles and inflicted some damage, but lost it in the mist.

Of the three bombs it had dropped, the first, an oil bomb, hit the boiler house at the northern end of the Hawker shed, splattering oil around without exploding. The second one buried itself in the dope shop floor, also without going off, and the third went through the roof at the southern end of the erecting shop, hitting a girder, which deflected it. Instead of penetrating the floor, it skidded along it, through a paint spray booth, killing one of the firm's cats en route, then through a toilet cubicle. It finally passed through the outer wall and finished up close to a semi-sunk shelter outside, confronting some Hawker staff as they emerged from it!

They were not the only ones close to the scene. George Edwards, then the Experimental Department Manager at Vickers, had also been nearer the action than he would have liked.

"I was in a hangar over the other side over which I'd laid claim for some reason - and one of the joys of wartime, of course, was that if you wanted something you went and took it - and I was over there alone. And all of a sudden all hell was let loose and there was another raid, and there were bombs thumping about and ack-ack. all over the shop, so when this had died down I sort of crawled out from under the bench where I'd hidden myself and went out through a little side door. There on the banking was a large bomb, and I swear it was sizzling as I looked at it! The chap had let go too low, had hit the banking, and it had skidded round it like it was a motorcar. So I nipped off sharpish and found a soldier."

The soldier he found was Lieutenant Patton, who had been brought from the Vickers factory on the back of a young worker's motorcycle. A call to Bomb Disposal had brought the reply that they could not come yet, which was hardly surprising as the number of unexploded bombs in Britain had peaked at 3,759 the previous day!

Apart from a couple of slight shock cases, there were no casualties. The burst oil bomb was clearly no longer a problem, but Hurricane production could not resume until both the high explosive bombs had been dealt with. The one in the dope shop floor was buried too deep for Patton to get at. However, the other, distorted and tailless after passing through the roof, lay on the concrete apron outside the shed and was accessible, although few would have dared to touch it. Some pieces of corrugated iron had come away from the roof and lay nearby, one with holes through it where it had been fixed to the roof. Lieutenant Patton described what happened next.

"On the way across the field I had observed a bomb crater not too far away from the bomb. I decided that the best thing to would be to get the bomb into this crater, because if it did go off, any blast would be directed upwards and it would probably not damage the Hurricane assembly building."

Patton is said to have been fearless to the point of being foolhardy, and perhaps he needed to be to command the men under him, but he was well aware of the danger of what he intended to do. The bomb's fuse might have been instantaneous or delayed-action, and as its mechanism could not be heard without the aid of a stethoscope there was no way of knowing whether the fuse had been put into operation. There was a risk that moving the bomb across the ground, however carefully, would start the fuse ticking, even if it had not been properly armed during the bomb's short descent and its skidding impact. Apart from the *Luftwaffe* armourers who had bombed-up the Ju88 that morning, no-one knew what time the fuse had been

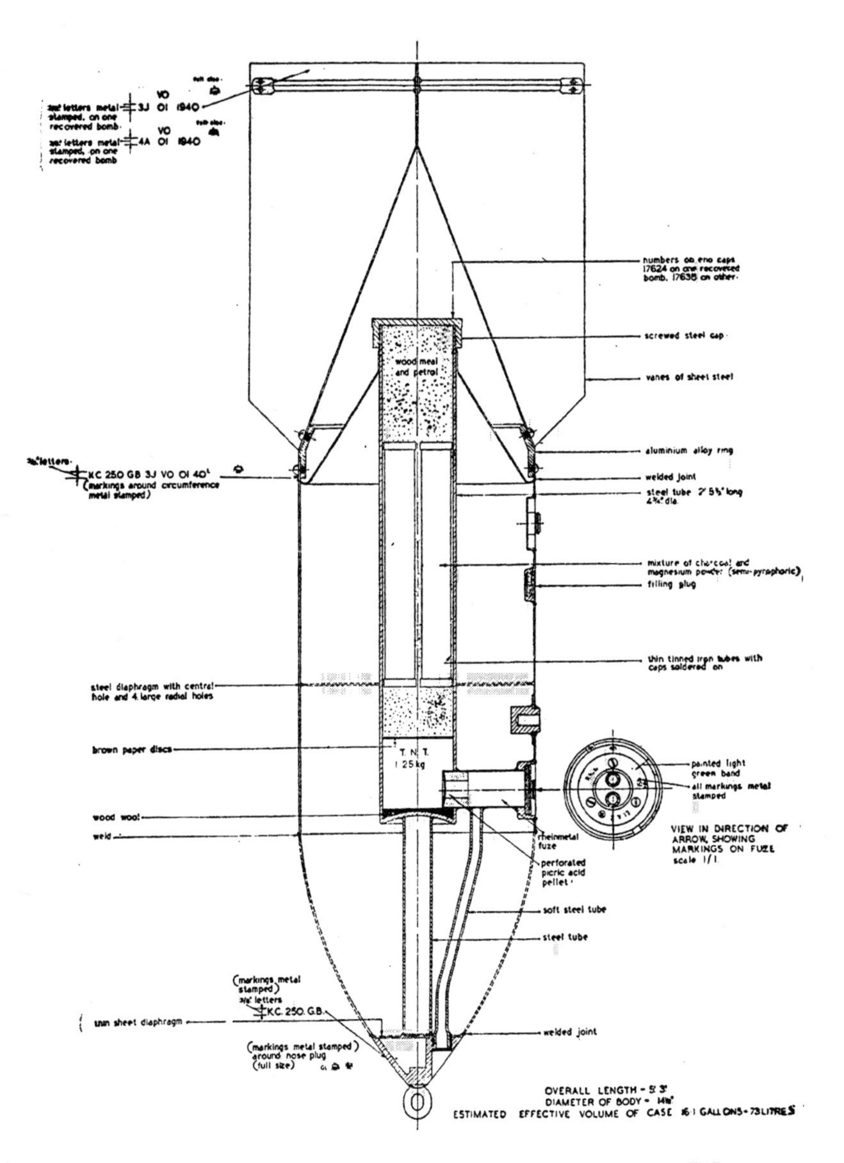

RECONSTRUCTION OF GERMAN OIL BOMB WITH H.E. BURSTER

set for. The bomb could, of course, have been made safe by the removal of the fuse, but this was impossible without specialised tools and knowledge. In addition, by now a booby-trapped fuse had been developed, which would explode the bomb if anyone attempted to tamper with it. Patton therefore had to weigh one risk against another. It would have been a greater danger - and been far more damaging - to have left the bomb lying by the Hawker shed.

The motorcyclist took Patton back to Vickers, where he found a piece of steel wire cable. He then commandeered a fifteen-hundredweight truck and its driver.

> "We drove to the scene and because the bomb had no fins and no way to attach the cable, I took the piece of corrugated iron, placed it alongside the bomb and gingerly rolled the bomb onto the centre of the corrugated sheet. The sheet was slightly concave in shape. I then passed the steel wire cable through the holes in the corrugated iron and tied the free end back on the cable."

By now Captain Douglas Cunnington, the 1st Battalion's adjutant, had arrived on the scene. One officer then attached the other end of the wire to the truck's tow-hook.

> "I got on the running-board on the driver's side and while watching the bomb had the driver move forward towards the bomb crater, then drive round its rim and to the other side."

This resulted in the bomb being at one side of the crater, the cable being stretched across it to the truck at the far side.

> "We then as gently as possible pulled the bomb to the rim of the crater and then gently pulled it forward until it slid down into the bottom of the crater......Then one of us untied the steel wire cable from the tow-hook and we all left as quickly as possible."

The Canadian sappers spent that night in Weybridge and moved on to do other work the next day. On that morning the bomb finally exploded, without any further damage to the Hawker shed. The fuse had been delayed-action, after all.

One threat had been averted, but there was still the question of the bomb in the dope shop floor. It was not until early in the afternoon of the 21st that a report of the Hawker incident was passed to 6th Bomb Disposal Company of the Royal Engineers, based at Reading. Lieutenant Davies, commanding 95, 96 and 97 Sections, was detailed to deal with it. He and his men worked from four in the afternoon until nine the next morning, when 47 Section - who had dealt with the St. George's Hill bomb in July - took over. Finally deciding that the bomb could not be recovered, the sappers built a 'chimney' of sandbags round it and the blast went out through the roof. Little further damage was caused.

On the 23rd a radio announcement was made by the King.

> "Many and glorious are the deeds of gallantry done during these perilous but famous days. In order that they should be worthily and promptly recognised I have decided to create at once a new mark of honour for men and women in all walks of civilian life. I propose to give my name to this new distinction, which will rank next to the Victoria Cross, and the George Medal for wider distribution."

These new decorations could also be awarded to servicemen and women for deeds of gallantry while not actually under fire.

Lieutenant Patton was awarded the George Cross and Captain Cunnington the George Medal. These were the first decorations awarded to the Canadian Army during the Second World War. The Vickers motorcyclist is said to have been awarded the MBE, while the truck driver received no recognition. His identity remains unknown - he was not one of Patton's sappers and presumably came from a British Army unit serving at Brooklands at that time. Possibly he considered that remaining alive after towing such a load was a reward in itself! It is worth bearing in mind that none of these men had any previous training or experience in Bomb Disposal work.

Chapter Seven
Home Fires

What by now had become known to the British public as 'the *Blitz*' continued, reaching new heights of intensity, although it was really a war of attrition and the exact opposite of the lightning tactics that had proved so successful on the Continent. Having been denied an expected easy victory by day, Göring's bombers now stepped up their night attacks, exploiting the RAF's lack of an effective night fighter force at this time. The days of quick victories were over and a gruelling siege had begun, with no result except to turn once-familiar streets into charred and smoking ruins. There would be little rest, except perhaps during the day, before nightfall and the next alert. It was a particularly frustrating time for the defenders, but occasionally a victory came their way.

24th September 1940

At 01.37 hours an He111 of *6/KG26*, with the gas works at Beckton in the East End as its target, strayed over Surrey. Shortly after the crew had dumped their bombs they were caught and illuminated by a searchlight from 460 Battery of the Royal Artillery, who were based in the Weybridge area at the time. Anti-aircraft gunners in the Slough area scored a direct hit, shooting off the Heinkel's tail. All four crewmen bailed out as the bomber broke up and caught fire, crashing and burning out near the Gordon Boys' Home at Chobham. Two minutes earlier their load had landed at the village of Bookham, demolishing a house.

For the crew this was the beginning of an eventful night. All were captured unhurt and subsequently interrogated. *Gefreiter* Werner Jenreck was escorted by troops of the searchlight battery from Byfleet police station and questioned at their headquarters by an RAF officer, one Flying Officer Miller from Fighter Command at Stanmore in Middlesex. Subsequently

Blitz or not, ordinary life had to continue. Here, milk is delivered to Primrose Road in Hersham, circa 1940. Note the gas mask in its case, ready for use. (Elmbridge Museum 212)

collected by a detachment from the 2nd Battalion of the Irish Guards, which as part of the 20th Guards Brigade were based at Woking, Jenreck joined his fellow crew members at Weybridge police station. Later that day the four men were removed under guard by the Brigade's headquarters personnel to the RAF's specialist interrogation centre at Cockfosters in north London.

Shocked by what had happened to them and naively believing Nazi propaganda about British concentration camps and firing squads - not to mention a possible lynching by bombed-out civilians - few newly shot-down aircrew were prepared for what really lay ahead. The interviewer would be superior in rank, often an aircrew member himself, and usually too old to play a more active part in the war. Fluent German was a necessity, as was patience, a good memory and a knowledge of human nature.

At this stage of the war the *Luftwaffe* was still confident of victory and therefore not as security-conscious as the RAF. A search of an airman's flying-suit pockets could reveal all kinds of interesting things, even if he had the sense to keep his mouth shut. Quite a few did not; careful questioning, a cigarette and an apparently sympathetic ear could also result in a good deal of useful information. This ranged from unit details to comments on the efficiency or otherwise of *Luftwaffe* radio navigation beams and the RAF's attempts to counter them. An interrogation could be very effective if it was conducted as soon as possible after the subject had been captured, especially in the small hours of the morning. Crew members were likely to compare notes once the questions ceased, and further information could be obtained by the simple method of putting them into a 'bugged' cell.

25/26th September 1940

At 22.30 hours six bombs fell at Foxwarren Farm in Redhill Road to the southeast of Brooklands. Some fifty incendiaries fell in Terrace Road near the Thames at 23.11 hours, being put out by the Fire Brigade and local troops. At 00.30 hours the next morning one oil and five HE bombs fell on open ground in the Brooklands House Estate, followed five minutes later by other incendiaries between Weybridge and Molesey. At 00.52 hours others fell at Field Common, with a further two on Council land at Weybridge at 01.22 hours. Finally, at 01.55 hours two incendiaries fell near a house in Station Avenue in Walton. Other bombs fell in Byfleet and Addlestone.

At 22.40 hours on the following evening six bombs fell next to a barrage balloon site in the grounds of Brooklands House, causing some shelter damage but no casualties.

27th September 1940

At 09.24 hours sixteen enemy aircraft in four diamond formations of four were turned back from London and approached Brooklands from the north. The Woburn Park gun site opened fire, quickly joined by that at Fairmile Common, which shot down a Ju88 of *2/KG77* at South Holmwood, near Dorking. One crewman was killed and three others baled out. Hurricanes of 1 (RCAF) and 303 (Polish) Squadrons also attacked, claiming this aircraft and a second Ju88 of *3/KG77*, which left the formation with both engines smoking and crashed near East Grinstead. One man died in this aircraft and three others baled out, but of these only one survived. The RAF lost a Hurricane of 303 Squadron, which crashed near Stoke D'Abernon. Its pilot,

BRITISH AIR SUPREMACY
WEYBRIDGE
AIRSCREW
BLADES
MANUFACTURED BY
The
AIRSCREW
Co. Ltd
WEYBRIDGE
ENGLAND
THE AIRSCREW CO. LTD., WEYBRIDGE ENGLAND
LONDON OFFICE · GROSVENOR GARDENS HOUSE · SW1

Pilot Officer W Zak, baled out but suffered burns. A Spitfire crashed near Walton station. It was thought to have been flown by Flight Sergeant Charles Sidney of 92 Squadron, who was killed.

This dogfight had an unexpected sequel in 1976, when the remains of the South Holmwood Ju88 were dug up and both engines recovered. One went to Canada and the other is now on display at Brooklands Museum.

The rest of the day was quiet, apart from a lone Bf110 that was engaged at midday by all the Weybridge gun sites and left trailing smoke from one engine.

28/29th September 1940

At 00.25 hours one bomb fell on Field Common, followed by three others in the Rydens Road area of Walton at 02.20. One landed at the corner of Normanhurst Road and Rydens Road. In so doing it showed the value of the Anderson shelter.

Named after the prewar Home Secretary, Andersons had been widely distributed at the start of the war, most being sited in back gardens, dug into the ground and consequently often prone to flooding. An apparently flimsy corrugated structure, the Anderson could withstand anything short of a direct hit. Here the occupants of one such shelter, situated twenty feet from the bomb's impact, were unharmed. A second bomb fell close to Selwyn Road and a third at the end of Florence Road in Walton. Ted Petty and his Home Guard friends had good cause to remember this one.

> "It showed the strange effect blast could have. The nearest house was a detached one, with the back door at the side, opening directly into the kitchen. The bomb blew the door inwards, with hardly a mark on it, and hung it neatly on a dresser. We tried to refit the door, but we couldn't get it to go back."

These three incidents seemed likely to be the result of a single raider dumping its load, and the nearby reservoirs provided as good an aiming mark as any. At 05.00 hours a further four bombs fell on land used by the Weylands sewage works at Weybridge. There were no casualties.

At 09.00 hours a lone Do17 flew through low cloud in an attempt to strafe the balloon barrage at Brooklands. Driven off

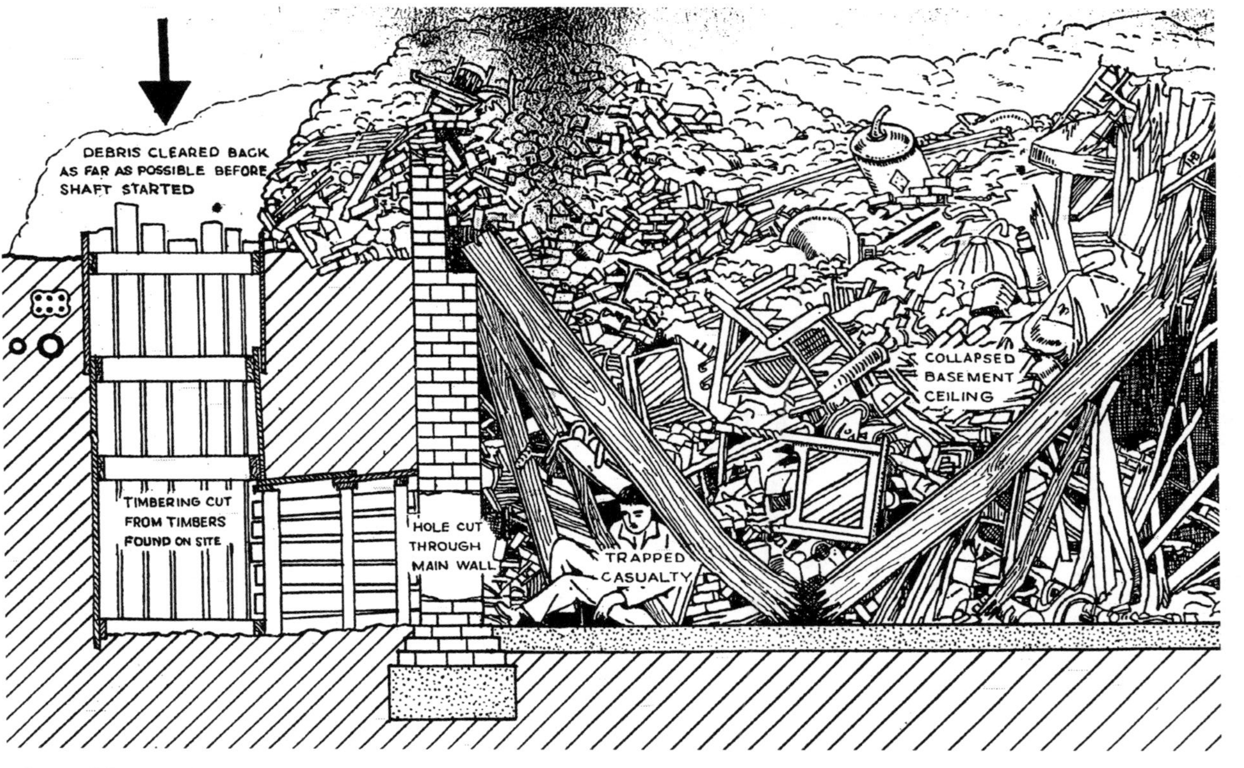

Part of Rescue Training Manual, showing a method of reaching survivors in a collapsed basement

by Bofors fire, it flew away, pursued by Hurricanes. A single Ju88 was seen high over the airfield at 10.22 hours, presumably on reconnaissance, and at 21.45 hours that night two oil bombs fell near a balloon site.

This was one of several incidents in an alert that lasted for some three hours and proved to be one of the heaviest raids that Weybridge had so far had to endure. Brooklands Road was blocked when twenty HE bombs and two hundred incendiaries fell near the Vickers works, although they caused no damage to it. Other bombs fell across Hersham, the main railway line to London, Falmouth and Burwood Roads. Again the Rydens Road area received its quota. Two unexploded bombs went off at different times, demolishing some houses that fortunately had been evacuated.

One house at the corner of Old Avenue and Queens Road was blasted into rubble by a direct hit, a fragment of which narrowly missed a man in a nearby cottage as he threw himself to the floor. Finally, at 00.25 hours the next morning twelve bombs fell across St. George's Hill from Cavendish Road to Cains Hill, blocking a road in that area.

Surprisingly, there were no casualties, although several people found themselves being accommodated by friends and neighbours. The East End evacuees must have concluded that there was no escape here either.

Although life was particularly precious now, it was inevitable that some people would place a high value on their property. In 1936 a dower house, formerly known as The Heath, had been converted into the Heath Hotel. It had a strongroom in the basement, and by 1940 this was being used by several friends of the Edwards family, who then owned it, to store valuables. The invasion threat, stories of German troops looting in Occupied Europe, and above all the bombing, showed this to be a wise decision. Several residents of St. George's Hill followed suit, and it proved a fortunate choice as the building survived, later becoming the Heath Club.

29th September 1940

At 16.45 hours one bomb fell near Weybridge station, a second near Whiteley and a third, an oil bomb, on the Heath near St.

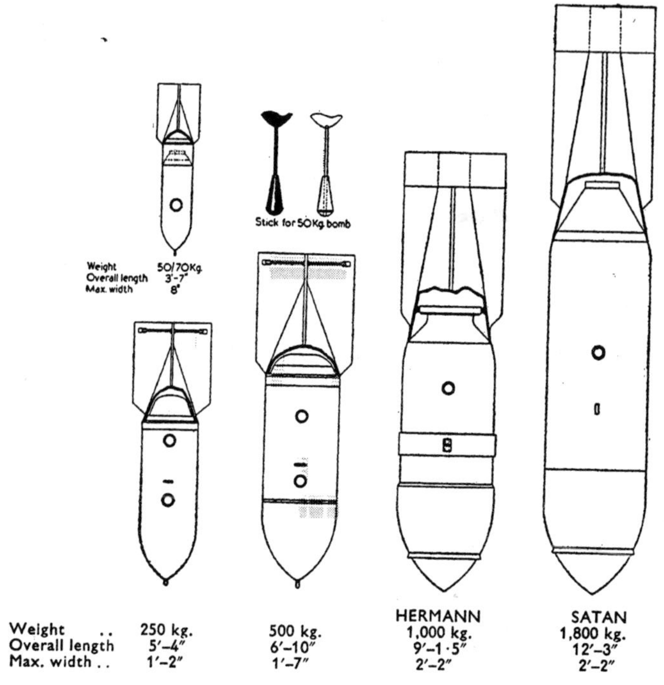

FIG. 2B.—GERMAN G.P. BOMB

The various types of German General Purpose (High Explosive) bombs. The 1,000 kg 'Hermann' will feature later in some detail.

George's Avenue. Damage was slight and there were no casualties. At 21.25 hours one oil and two HE bombs fell close to the junction of Brooklands and Byfleet Roads and at 23.50 others fell in Molesey Road. One bomb fell within thirty feet of a public shelter, but fortunately the occupants were unharmed. A house in Molesey Road was destroyed, resulting in five deaths, and an Anderson was stove in when it took a direct hit from an oil bomb, killing two people and injuring a third.

30th September 1940

At 02.38 hours one bomb severely damaged a house in Old Avenue on St. George's Hill, although there were no casualties, while at 02.45 an oil bomb fell on a tennis court, also on St. George's Hill, causing a slight fire that was soon controlled.

Another four bombs were reported during the day, one at Walton at 1314 and three others at a reservoir there.

1st October 1940

At 01.35 hours one oil bomb fell near the water reservoir on St. George's Hill and failed to ignite, like so many of its kind. Five minutes later three bombs fell on open ground near the Vickers factory, without casualties or damage.

1st/2nd October 1940

Between 21.15 and 00.24 hours thirty-eight HE bombs fell in the district, ten of them across Burhill golf course. Others landed at Hersham, at Cains Hill and on the railway line, dislocating the branch line service to Addlestone. Seventeen bombs fell at 0024 in the middle of Walton, temporarily blocking the High Street with debris. One removed the entire front of a house in Ashley Park Avenue. Fortunately the occupants had slept in another room and were unharmed. Not so lucky were those who lived in Rylton House, a block of flats opposite the Council offices. Two people were killed and two others injured when three flats in the building's south wing were destroyed.

The local United Dairies depot was hit, with the loss of four horses, although the occupants of a sandbagged shelter twelve feet from the explosion survived. The last bomb landed in Sidney Road, damaging the front of a house. It was noted the next morning that a notice on the front gate appealing for the local Spitfire Fund was unscathed!

3rd October 1940

At 16.50 hours a Do17 approached Brooklands from the southeast. It did not bomb, but strafed a balloon without destroying it. Two Bofors guns and one Lewis gun fired back before the Dornier disappeared in low cloud and mist.

4th October 1940

At 20.35 hours a wandering barrage balloon trailed over Weybridge and grounded in St George's Avenue, having damaged several roofs and chimneypots en route. Then at 21.17 one hundred incendiaries and three HE bombs fell on Field Common, causing slight damage but no casualties.

While an area might have only one 'incident' during a night, *Luftwaffe* tactics were to send small numbers of aircraft over in waves. This kept the alert going for long periods, resulting in idle factories and loss of sleep. It was in contrast to the mass raids later to be inflicted on Germany by Bomber Command.

8th October 1940

At 21.55 hours four HE bombs and some fifty incendiaries fell near Caesar's Camp on St. George's Hill. One of these did not explode until the following afternoon. Two other unexploded bombs were found at Burhill and Field Common during the day, presumably left over from the raid of six days before.

9th October 1940

During the morning the possibility of storms caused the balloon barrage to be hauled down and, at 10.05 hours, two Ju88s took advantage of this. The first attacked from the north at 6,000 feet, but flew off to the east on meeting heavy defending fire. The second then approached from the northwest, dodging in and out of the clouds, with shells bursting behind it. The Parachute-and-Cable detachment fired two rockets, but these proved to be defective. The Ju88 then dived and dropped its load, which overshot the Vickers factory and landed in the woods on St. George's Hill, damaging one house. The light machine guns on top of the main Vickers office block fired back, sending the Ju88 off to the east trailing smoke. There were no casualties, but one Vickers toolmaker, Robbie Bolton, had good cause to remember this attack.

> "The alert had sounded and we all ran across the road to the shelters. As I ran I saw what looked like rain hitting the ground and realized that couldn't be right - it was a fine day. Then I looked up, and there was a Junkers 88 just sitting above us! He strafed us as he passed over the works. One of the managers and his girlfriend were running in front of me and the burst only just missed them!"

10th October 1940

At 22.10 hours one hundred incendiaries fell in the Molesey Road area, with four bombs at Field Common. There was slight damage, but no casualties.

12th October 1940

Three bombs fell in the Bessborough Reservoir at 22.27 hours, with no casualties.

A look through Anti-Aircraft Command's records at this time shows that raiders approaching the capital from the southwest were by now taking a fairly predictable route, although the defences were not yet sufficiently well organized to take advantage of this. Using the Solent and the Hamble estuary as an unmistakable navigation checkpoint, they headed north, turning again in the Weybridge area to fly east towards London along the Thames. Judging by the number of bombs being dropped around them, there seemed little doubt that the reservoirs between Walton and the Thames were also being used as markers on the way in. However some people believed that the shape of the reservoirs resembled Brooklands track and misled German bomb aimers. Certainly, looking at a modern map of the area, the adjacent Knights and Bessborough Reservoirs form an irregular oval not unlike the shape of the track as it then was. Ted Petty recalled that many incendiaries, with just a few high explosive bombs, fell in that area.

Containers, which held fifty or more incendiary bombs each, were frequently dropped from *Luftwaffe* aircraft. Small bursting charges operated at a pre-set height, opening the containers and releasing their contents over a wide area. They were often called 'Molotov Breadbaskets' by the British public - a nickname that had originated during the war between Finland and the Soviet Union in 1939-40. Again Ted Petty was a little closer to the action than he would have preferred.

> "We'd get baskets of incendiaries come down and a lot wouldn't open - if they hit water they made a hell of a splash. Part of my job in the Home Guard was to damp down fires. You'd knock off work at eight at night, go home to Mum's tea, and she'd say to you; 'Are you going out tonight?' 'No, I'm not.' Then the siren would go and you'd be off. I used to cycle over to Walton - I was one of those who sat on top of the gasometer, putting out incendiaries with a sandbag! On top of a gasometer! I can't imagine a more stupid place to be. You'd do all kinds of daft things, get home at about four in the morning and then get up for work at eight. And it wasn't just for a night or two - this went on for weeks. How we did it on just one egg, a piece of cheese and a couple of rashers of bacon I don't know."

Sometimes the incendiaries went out of their own accord, but

An Armstrong-Whitworth Whitley V, similar to the 10 Squadron aircraft that crashed at Hanger Hill on the night of 14th October.

there were other dangers.

> "One night I was cycling to the command post during an incendiary raid, and it was as light as day. All of a sudden they all went out, and because of the blackout I hit the kerb and went flying!"

Apart from the disruption and damage they caused, it is possible that incendiaries were dropped by some of the more experienced crews to serve as navigation beacons for the others to follow. The array of coloured marker flares, which the RAF would use with such devastating effect over German cities, was not yet available to either side.

14th October 1940

In the early hours of the morning a Bristol Beaufighter of 219 Squadron, lost and short of fuel, crashed at the village of Send, near Woking, after both the crewmen had safely baled out. A Ju88 passed over Brooklands at 13.08 hours. That evening the RAF was to lose a bomber at Weybridge, in an incident well remembered by those who witnessed it.

At this time RAF Bomber Command was waging a war on two fronts. The first was over Germany itself. The second was to attempt to destroy or to disrupt the build-up of invasion barges in the French and Belgian ports across the Channel. That afternoon orders were issued to the crews of 10 Squadron, based at Leeming in Yorkshire, to attack two targets. Most of the aircraft were to raid Stettin in the Baltic, but three crews were detailed to attack a barge concentration at Le Havre.

This squadron formed part of Bomber Command's No.4 Group. It was equipped with the Armstrong Whitworth Whitley Mark V, a twin-engined bomber of angular design, with a slab-sided fuselage, thick wings and a twin-tail. Too slow for daylight operations, the Whitley had taken part in night leaflet raids during the early part of the war. Although dubbed 'The Flying Barn Door' and 'The Old Lady' by those who flew it, it was generally regarded as a tough and reliable aircraft.

The three crews bound for Le Havre were given a course from Leeming to Finningley in the southern part of Yorkshire, from there to Harwell and out over the coast at Bognor Regis, returning by the same route. Two Whitleys returned safely, but the third, flown by Sergeant Wright and his crew, did not.

Although the balloons stationed around Brooklands may have seemed comical to those on the ground who knew little of their purpose, to aircrew they were anything but funny. While the balloon itself was an obvious obstacle, even worse was the cable that secured it, for this could saw into and even sever an aircraft's wing. Twenty-four balloons surrounded Brooklands at this time and each had its own numbered site. Site 21 was in the grounds of Brooklands House, near Weybridge station and to the north of the airfield.

Sergeant Wright's Whitley took off from Leeming at 17.31 hours. Of its five-man crew, which included a trainee second pilot, none were completely green. Some had taken part in the first Berlin raids the previous summer. Wright was however a little less experienced than his fellow crewmen and had only recently become a bomber captain.

At the gun sites in the Weybridge area, the detachments settled down to another long and weary night. Although the sky was bright and moonlit, from now on the only illumination they would see would come from the searchlights nearby, or from the flash of their own shells when the next alert sounded.

In its flight south, the Whitley may have strayed off course by just a few degrees. If so, this would have been enough to avoid one prohibited area - the Inner Artillery Zone over London - but not enough to be clear of the Weybridge defences. By now a considerable raid was in progress over London, with many large visible fires. Just before 20.00 hours the engines of the Whitley could be heard as, apparently lost, it groped its way through the sky just to the north of Brooklands, close to Site 21. Clearly aware of the danger he was in, Wright used the aircraft's Verey pistol to fire a correct recognition signal.

Ernest Babb, on his way with friends to the Vickers night shift, later remembered them cheering when they saw what they took to be a German bomber fall from the sky and crash near Weybridge station. Delighted that the gunners were finally doing their job, he went into work, and was considerably shaken when he learned the truth the next day. Doctor Beare, a local GP, went to the crash scene, but took his time, as his own son was a prisoner-of-war, and not surprisingly he had come to hate the Germans. His feelings when he discovered a dead RAF airman on a road near the crash can well be imagined. All five men had died, accompanied by a series of explosions as some bombs went off. The ARP at Walton informed RAF Kenley, who in turn passed on the news to No.4 Group.

The Whitley had struck Site 21's balloon cable, severing part of one wing, which landed in the garden of a house at Weybridge Park. The tail unit and rear gun turret fell onto a house named Elgin Lodge, in Elgin Road, and the remainder crashed nearby at Hanger Hill, in a wood close to the station. The balloon, freed when the cable snapped, drifted away.

Not all the bombs had gone off, however. Dick Lewis was one of several schoolboys who saw them the next morning, lying in the wreckage. A Bomb Disposal unit later dealt with them, and an RAF crane recovered whatever could be salvaged.

The subsequent inquiry found that a fire had begun in the centre of the bomber's fuselage when the incendiaries it was carrying ignited. The cause of the fire, if it was ever established, was not mentioned on the aircraft's accident card. Given that the Luftwaffe was active that night, it is possible - although it has been hotly denied by some local people - that the Whitley may have been accidentally fired on by the London defences. At least two witnesses have said that the bomber was on fire before it crashed, and it seems unlikely that this would have occurred solely by hitting the cable. Also, given that the cable snapped after severing the wing, what was it that caused the Whitley's tail to break away as well?

Just before the crash the Whitley apparently dropped a flare, which was said to have fallen onto a balloon and destroyed it. Curiously, there is no mention of a balloon loss in the records of 954 Squadron for this night. It seems that either Wright was trying to establish his position, or else he had realized there was a fire in the bomb-bay and he was trying to save his crew's lives by dumping the incendiaries. The anti-aircraft gunners might well have mistaken the twin-tailed silhouette for that of a Do17, especially if it appeared to be dropping flares near Brooklands, as German aircraft had recently done.

Someone who was also a victim of this crash was Mr Thomas Dickson, then eighty-one and a retired company chairman, who lived with his wife, a nurse and domestic staff at Elgin Lodge. His account, written three days later, is reproduced here by permission of his family, and gives a good idea of the routine of their life at that stage of the war.

> "At Elgin Lodge we have so far been fortunate in escaping any injury by the enemy bombers, although every night they make great efforts all round us to get armament works near this. However, on Monday the 14th the house was severely damaged, not by the enemy, but, alas, by one of our own bombers. Mrs Dickson, Miss Niven and I dine at seven pm. The enemy is generally overhead by seven-thirty. We had finished and were in the drawing-room before a good fire. We usually, when the explosions get dangerously near, shut up and retire to our cellar shelter, where we are safe against anything but a direct hit, and sleep in good cabin bunks with the staff: five in all. We were just deciding to get down to our shelter when there was a fearful crash, with a crescendo of falling glass, and the whole house trembled. We all got down to the shelter in thirty seconds and waited, while bomb after bomb exploded close by. After ten minutes the explosions ceased and the parlour maid, who is fearless, went up to see what had happened. She came back and waved her hand to me, but said nothing.
>
> "I went upstairs to the large bedroom, where Mrs Dickson and I sleep in peacetime. The door could only be opened a few inches, but enough to show me the room piled with wreckage, a large hole in the ceiling and floor above, and a larger one in the roof above that, with the moon shining in a clear sky. As there had been no explosion in the house, I concluded that a delayed-action bomb had struck us. I at once went out to get help and luckily found a flight lieutenant and three Army officers and a couple of cars waiting at the end of Elgin Road. They offered their services, and one of the RAF men said he would have a look outside before going upstairs, produced his torch, and in a moment said, 'Well, you have had an escape, your house has been hit by an aeroplane, and only the lightest part of it.'"

Small, but deadly. A German incendiary bomb. (IWM D3534)

What follows next may not be correct, since no other witness mentioned engine trouble.

"Next day we learned what had happened. A British Whitley two-engined bomber had evidently left to attack the French coast, but developed engine trouble which forced the pilot to return without dropping his bombs. He was seen in difficulties, flying low round St. George's Hill, evidently seeking a

> landing place. Unfortunately, he fouled a balloon cable, dropped both wings in different places; engines and bombs fell on the commons, burnt themselves out and exploded the bombs. The tailpiece and turret with four machine guns and full load of cartridges carried on and cut into the Elgin Lodge roof, scraped off the turret guns and cartridges, weighing nearly a ton, leaving it on Mrs Dickson's bed, and landed on the tennis court, carrying the drawing-room verandah with it. The crew of five were all killed. They hadn't a dog's chance; they were too low down to allow their parachutes to open and their dead bodies were found in various directions.
>
> "Sentries were put on the wreckage at once. The corporal slept in a chair in the hall. Next morning, from daylight numberless inspectors, officers, wardens and others came to look at the wreckage. It was only then that the machine was identified and it was not until the same evening that the last of the dead was found."

The process of clearing up the battered remains of Elgin Lodge began on the 17th.

> "Today the RAF salvage officers and men arrived from Slough and have been dismantling, collecting, packing and laying out every nut, bolt and instrument. The turret, a mass of intricate machinery, is being cut and dismembered piece by piece; belts containing thousands of unexploded cartridges and four machine guns packed into sacks and hoisted from off Mrs Dickson's bed, to be lowered from the window. It is rather a sad business to find gauntlets, oxygen masks, emergency rations belonging to the dead crew with their names on them among the wreckage."

The house was patched up by means of a large tarpaulin to cover the gaping hole in the roof, but the elderly owners must have been chilled to the bone during the winter that followed, especially as heating fuel was rationed. On top of all this was the long separation that total war inevitably brings. Mr Dickson's three sons were not in a position to help as one was suffering from wounds received at Dunkirk, while the other two were serving in North Africa and Ceylon. During June 1941 Mr Dickson rose suddenly from his bed when the sirens sounded and died of a stroke. Although a veteran of the Boer and First World Wars, the strain of this new kind of warfare had proved too much for him.

Why did the Whitley get so far off track? It was the opinion of the officer commanding No.4 Group that Sergeant Wright was map-reading, mistook his navigation beacons and changed course too soon. This, however, is a mystery unlikely to be solved. Wright's crew took the secrets of their last flight with them. It was the first, though sadly not the last, instance of the Brooklands balloons helping to bring down one of their own aircraft. Having said that, it is only fair to point out that the balloon crews were not at fault.

Elgin Lodge was later demolished and the site is occupied today by a block of flats.

16th October 1940

One HE bomb fell at Walton at 21.50 hours, causing some damage and one slight casualty.

17th October 1940

Between 19.30 and 20.00 hours several bombs fell at Rydens Road, Normanhurst Road, King George Avenue and The Furrows. One at King George Avenue hit a shelter, whose occupants had a narrow escape when it failed to go off!

These all fell in a stick that nearly straddled a nearby searchlight site, leading to renewed complaints concerning the location of it. The loss of sleep due to bombs and gunfire was something that had to be wearily accepted, but many people were sure that this light was attracting bombs to an area of Walton that had already had more than enough. Other bombs fell at Terrace Road, causing five casualties, none of which were serious.

19th October 1940

One oil bomb fell in a field off Burhill and a second one hit a house in Oatlands Close, landing in the attic, although most of the burning contents went down the outside of the roof. There was one slight injury. At 23.50 hours six bombs fell across the Thames from Oatlands Drive to Sunbury. The third of these exploded in the river, narrowly missing Walton Bridge, which due to damage had to be replaced after the war had ended.

21st October 1940

At 17.51 hours the Bofors detachment on St. George's Hill glimpsed an He111 through a gap in the clouds and fired on it without effect. Earlier, at 13.40 hours, one bomb had exploded in the garden of a house to the west of Cavendish Road, blasting a crater fifty feet wide and fifteen feet deep. There were no casualties. A few seconds later two other bombs, probably dropped from the same aircraft, fell harmlessly on open ground south of Cains Hill.

22nd October 1940

An oil bomb fell near Terrace Road at 19.45 hours, causing no damage or casualties.

26th October 1940

At 13.30 hours a single Ju88 approached Brooklands, and for its pains met heavy gunfire, which drove it off. The bomber was chased away to the west by three Hurricanes, but it evidently got away from them as it was later seen on its own over Farnborough.

27th October 1940

A bomb fell in a thicket near the Portsmouth Road at 04.20 hours, but failed to explode. An HE bomb fell nearby and another at Foxwarren Farm. There was some minor damage but no casualties.

Throughout the war, and particularly at this time, unexploded bombs proved a hazard, not only to those people who literally stumbled across them, but also to small boys who went out looking for them and often took them home as souvenirs. Most were too heavy for even an adult to move, and in addition their weight meant that they were often deeply embedded in the ground, leaving nothing more than a deceptively small hole to mark their arrival. However, incendiaries, being lighter, were frequently found scattered on the surface. As some civilians regarded tackling incendiaries with stirrup pumps and sand-bags as something of a new sport, so the Germans added an extra element to the game by booby-trapping these small weapons with explosive charges. Still, most children imagined themselves to be immortal, and for many, especially those who had been evacuated to the countryside, the war was the ultimate, madly exciting game. Stern lectures and corporal punishment by teachers and parents meant little. If you had a collection of war souvenirs you were somebody, especially if any of them were German and you had incurred some risk to get your hands on them.

Algy Allington was one boy who never forgot an incendiary bomb that he picked up.

> "It was about a foot long. I put it in my jacket and took it to a boys' club. We used to defuse them with a key, but we couldn't do anything with this one, so I took it outside, threw it against a wall and it promptly exploded!"

In spite of taking chances like this, he survived. Unexploded anti-aircraft shells returning to earth were another problem. They were supposed to self-destruct before doing so, but not all did, and to this day one is said to be buried in the Members' Banking area of Brooklands. Occasionally RAF bombs were jettisoned or fell from aircraft in the wrong places. These were removed by Bomb Disposal squads from a variety of odd locations, including at least one from Walton police station. It seems likely that some public-spirited, not to say lucky, citizen had picked it up and handed it to the duty sergeant!

There were other ways in which the police could be involved, as 'Boyd' Kelly's future brother-in-law found out.

> "I remember an incendiary landing in the front garden of my wife-to-be. I covered that one with soil. Then her younger brother found one in a garden at New Haw. He proudly brought it home and was fined ten shillings in court three days later for not having handed it in!"

It was not only souvenir-hunting civilians who found themselves dealing with bombs. The Home Guard, deprived of any invading parachutists to apprehend, often found themselves acting as an extension of the ARP. The following account first appeared in the Apprentice Club Journal, published by Vickers in 1945 and retailing at one shilling and sixpence (7.5p). Entitled *Never In Action, Never Defeated*, it was written by one J A Froude, apparently a former Home Guard officer. Although names were altered or deleted and locations not given, it gives a good idea of how things could be in 1940-41. Some nights were routine, but others were definitely not.

> "One of the more unpleasant Home Guard institutions was 'Guard Night', the routine of which was always the same. If parade was at 20.00 hours, the first arrivals at 20.30 were the two rookies of the section, driving either their late 1939 Rolls-Royce or their 24 hp Packard. They were followed at regular intervals by the other ranks in Fords and Austins, the NCOs on bicycles and old Lieutenant G on shank's pony at 21.00 hours. Then the event of the evening - the arrival of Sergeant H with the BEER. Nothing, not even the mounting of the guard, or an air raid, could interfere with the

ritual of the arrival of this precious fluid, which was conveyed tenderly to the guardroom for future use. At two in the morning, in an atmosphere you could cut with a knife, with a pack of well-thumbed cards and the wine flowing freely, the section would be well away, but here comes the rub, the homeward trek in the bleary morn. It's really amazing how one can soak in all this blarney about the fresh sparkling dawn, the clear morning air and the sun rising in all its glory, until one actually has to creep home at five in the morning. Even if the sun is rising, one doesn't notice it. One is usually very stiff, very damp and very, very cold. There is only one place to be at this time in the morning, and that is BED."

On the nights when action did occur, these discomforts would be replaced by others.

"The night of the air raid saw the section at its very best. Several shops and a small pub were fired by incendiaries and the section was well to the fore, salvaging a prodigious quantity of Brown Ale and Booth's Dry Gin. Our squad was then rushed to the churchyard to deal with more incendiaries that were falling and had set fire to the roof of the church. Three of our bravest warriors climbed to the roof of a small outhouse to extinguish burning embers which were threatening to fire it. After three or four minutes, all three fell with a loud crash through the roof of the hut, smashing the thing to smithereens.

"A chain bucket party, after passing their buckets around a complete circle several times in the murky darkness, discovered their error and began a gallant assault upon the smouldering rafters of the church. A mass of khaki-clad figures fought their way unsteadily up a swaying and ancient ladder, clutching buckets of water which slopped unpleasantly on the unfortunates below. The little liquid that did reach the top was thrown upon the flames, with the exception of one bucketful, complete with bucket, which fell upon the upturned face of the vicar, the Rev. Septimus Piffle, who was directing operations from below. Our only casualty of note was dear old Alfie G, who disappeared through an insecure portion of the ladder, and was discovered at the crack of dawn slumbering peacefully in the tomb of Lord Bottle of Hooch - one of our more renowned local corpses. Having removed Corporal Harris and Private Mickey A, and a goodly quantity of empty quart bottles from the belfry, the section gathered up its goods and chattels, and withdrew in good order."

It is easy to see where the inspiration for the BBC series *Dad's Army* came from. Certainly Captain Mainwaring would not have been amused!

28th October 1940

Several bombs fell across Walton and Hersham at 02.15 hours. Two landed in Sidney Road, one of them just five yards from a shelter. A third fell at Rydens Road and a fourth at Walton

Road Nurseries. Two others fell harmlessly on open ground east of Molesey Road. At 19.05 hours that evening one bomb fell in the Field Common area.

1st November 1940

This night had several incidents, some of which bordered on the farcical. At 20.50 hours one heavy bomb fell on Terrace Road, blowing a crater forty feet wide by fifteen feet deep, into which a small car promptly drove, although the occupants escaped with nothing more than bruises. A dozen nearby houses received blast damage. Another bomb fell in a smallholding at the back of Terrace Road, damaging hen-houses and beehives. Police and wardens had a lively time rounding up the escaped livestock, no doubt collecting a few stings in the process! A woman living nearby was heard loudly proclaiming that Hitler had killed her husband's goat, but nevertheless the animal was found, grazing peacefully as if nothing had happened. At 22.05 hours three bombs, two of which failed to go off, fell between Queens Road and Walton station.

2nd November 1940

At 00.15 hours one oil and two HE bombs fell in the woods at Burwood Park, causing some slight bomb damage but no casualties. That evening at 20.22 hours several bombs and many incendiaries fell across Hersham. One hundred and fifty incendiaries came down at South Weylands Farm. Two people died when a bomb hit a pair of semi-detached houses at West Grove. A woman, suffering from shock and bruises, was dug out from under a pile of debris by a rescue party, who had to work in almost total darkness. They were lucky, for just after she was taken to hospital the whole of the house's upper floor collapsed. Another bomb fell on the footpath at Clarence Road, causing widespread house damage but no further casualties.

3rd November 1940

An He111, plotted by Fighter Command as Raid 67H, came in over Bognor Regis and flew over London, then circled Brooklands from 13.35 to 14.00 hours. The Parachute-and-Cable detachment were unable to fire any rockets as the Heinkel did not cross their lines. Although this crew's conduct showed that they were both persistent and aggressive, they evidently did not risk an attack on the airfield because of the balloon cables. The bomber presented only a fleeting target, taking cover in the clouds when it was fired on, and itself firing machine gun bullets apparently at random, one of which went through the window of a house at Hersham Road in Walton.

The Heinkel finally flew off towards Farnborough, then turned south and strafed the RAF Coastal Command base at Thorney Island as it recrossed the Sussex coast.

5th November

At 00.10 hours five bombs fell at Desborough Cut and fifty minutes later two more landed on the Weybridge Cricket Common, near a warden's post. A third hit a gravestone in Weybridge Cemetery. The 'victim' here had been the grandfather of schoolboy Dick Lewis, who had witnessed the aftermath of the 4th September raid.

> "Later in the war they replaced his headstone, but there are no longer any remains there. You can still see lumps of shrapnel in the surrounding headstones."

5/6th November 1940

The Fairmile Common and Wisley Common gun sites were in action overnight for several hours, providing a rather more elaborate type of firework display. One unexploded bomb was reported at Walton and two bombs fell on Weybridge Common, causing slight property damage. Another six fell at Addlestone, slightly damaging a farm.

6th November 1940

At 21.45 hours an oil bomb fell harmlessly near Burwood Park. An hour later eight bombs fell almost parallel to the river Mole, close to the Woburn Park gun site. Later, at 23.55 hours, a further stick of eight bombs fell from Paines Hill Park, Cobham, across the Portsmouth and Seven Hills Roads. One woman was injured and there was some blast damage.

7th November 1940

At one minute after midnight six bombs fell on St. George's Hill, causing some splinter damage but no casualties. At 12.06 hours

'Pottergate', in Rydens Avenue, Walton, photographed in June 1941 after repair work following a direct hit on the night of 9th November 1940. The owner and his daughter were visiting his wife in hospital at the time. 'Frensham' on the right, was almost completely demolished, although there were no casualties. (Elmbridge Museum)

a single Messerschmitt, reported as a Bf109 fighter, but more likely to have been a Bf110 reconnaissance aircraft, was plotted as Raid 18. It approached Weybridge, but turned away and was reported shot down by RAF fighters in Richmond Park. There was an error, for no such loss took place.

9th November 1940

Eight bombs fell between Rydens Avenue and the Mole at 19.30 hours, one making a direct hit on a pair of semi-detached houses, leaving only the rear outer wall standing. One householder and his wife had been sitting in the back room at the time. They were all smothered in dirt and plaster, but were saved when the inner edge of the bedroom floor above sagged over them, so forming a triangular space and deflecting debris from the upper storey towards the front of the house. The adjoining property was unoccupied. Other bombs fell at Rydens and Molesey Roads.

10th November

One bomb, part of a stick dropped across the Mole, fell in the Weybridge district at 19.57 hours, causing no damage or casualties.

11th November 1940

At 15.53 hours an enemy aircraft, variously described as a Do17, a Do215 or a Ju88 - which says little for the aircraft recognition standards of those on duty - approached the Fairmile Common gun site from the southeast. Seen briefly through low cloud and heavy rain, it was fired on and responded by dropping several bombs close to the site.

The raider then approached Brooklands, running through a barrage of Lewis and Bofors fire. The rain again caused several Bofors shells to prematurely explode. A line of nine rockets was fired by the Parachute-and-Cable detachment, but the bomber flew just above them as they reached their full height and the parachutes blossomed. No more bombs fell and the aircraft flew off to the south.

13th November 1940

All four heavy gun sites went into action at 13.24 hours, causing three Ju88s to take cover in cloud. Two of them reappeared six minutes later, turning south when fired on again. The third was then engaged again, this time with two Bofors sites joining in as well, and it climbed back into the clouds.

The Council fire-float and its crew, who were in action on the night of 29th November 1940. (Elmbridge Museum 122. 1989)

14/15th November 1940

On this night the *Luftwaffe* mounted *Operation Moonlight Serenade* - a major and devastating attack on the Midlands city of Coventry. Weather conditions were excellent for navigation and the operation's codename proved highly appropriate. Some bombers passed within range of the Fairmile Common gun site, which fired intermittently and without effect until 05.05 hours on the 15th.

At 19.30 hours on the following evening the three hundredth HE bomb to land in this part of Surrey hit a house at Dorney Grove in Weybridge. It was fortunate that the family who lived there were away at the time. Two others fell in the area, one of these into the Thames. An oil bomb fell harmlessly onto farmland.

16th November 1940

At 04.10 hours one heavy bomb fell by the river Mole. In the morning an unexploded bomb turned up in the garden of a house in Cavendish Road on St. George's Hill.

19th November 1940

An enemy aircraft was engaged by the Slough guns before flying over Brooklands at 01.42 hours. Several bombs were dropped, one of which fell near the Hawker assembly shed, but did no damage. At 07.20 hours that morning two bombs exploded harmlessly on open ground near Terrace Road.

23rd November 1940

At 00.20 hours nine bombs fell between Byfleet and the Seven Hills Road, with a hundred incendiaries on the Paines Hill Estate, one of these being estimated as the thousandth of its type to fall in the district. Fifteen minutes later one heavy HE bomb fell near the headquarters of 20th Guards Brigade on St. George's Hill, making a crater thirty feet in diameter.

28th November 1940

At 22.20 hours one heavy bomb fell in a house garden at Baker Street in Weybridge, blowing an unoccupied Anderson shelter over two gardens and onto the roof of an adjacent house. A second landed harmlessly in the same area, followed by some two hundred and fifty incendiaries scattered in the Brooklands-Queens Road-Seven Hills area. One house was all but gutted, although the owner and his staff, with assistance from the Fire Brigade, local wardens and some Army signallers who were stationed in the vicinity, salvaged most of the contents. One member of the 109th Heavy Anti-Aircraft Regiment was killed when another cluster of incendiaries fell on the Woburn Park gun site.

29/30th November 1940

At 21.00 hours one bomb demolished two houses at Carlton Road in Walton, leaving only one kitchen standing, in which a couple survived by diving under the table. Two other people, who had recently moved there after being bombed out elsewhere, died instantly. Many other houses were damaged and a hundred people made temporarily homeless.

Forty minutes later some one hundred incendiaries set fire to a bungalow on the tow-path near the Weir Hotel at Walton, the blaze being quickly extinguished by the Council's fire-float. At

22.05 hours one bomb fell at Apps Court Farm, then at 22.30 a further one hundred and fifty incendiaries landed at the junction of Brooklands and Byfleet Roads. Sixteen bombs fell between Foxwarren Farm and St. George's Hill golf club. Finally, just after midnight two more bombs fell in the Field Common area, injuring two civilians by shrapnel.

1st December 1940

A single Ju88, presumably on reconnaissance, was seen at 5,000 feet near Weybridge at 15.25 hours, although this time both sides decided to hold their fire.

3rd December 1940

At this time 253 Squadron were still at Kenley, and their Blue Section, consisting of three Hurricanes, was scrambled during the early afternoon with orders to climb to 10,000 feet. They were directed over London's Inner Artillery Zone, but found no 'trade' there and were redirected after a second enemy plot reported over southwest London. When over Weybridge at 12,000 feet, just before 14.15 hours, a Do17Z was seen, seven miles away and 2,000 feet lower.

Flying Officer Edwards, the section leader, attacked first, and return fire from the rear gunner was immediately silenced. Sergeant Cooper then followed, firing all his ammunition from an optimistic five hundred yards to one hundred. At this point his windscreen iced up and he did not see the results of his fire. Sergeant Whitehead then took over, attacking from the bomber's port quarter and pouring all his ammunition into it.

By now the Dornier was losing height and it went into a cloudbank as Whitehead ceased firing. Skimming the surface of the cloud at 7,000 feet, Edwards continued to chase the Dornier as it headed south, catching up with it as they neared the coast. He then fired the last of his ammunition from dead astern at no more than one hundred yards, seeing pieces fly off his target, which was now also trailing white smoke. Blue Section turned for home, frustrated at being able to claim only a damaged aircraft instead of a definite kill. However, on this day a Dornier 17Z of *5/KG2* crashed while trying to land at the *Luftwaffe* airfield at Estaires, killing everyone on board. This may have been due to Blue Section's attacks.

By chance a woman living in Walton had to go to hospital after being hit by a stray bullet from this action, even though it had started several miles from her home area. Considering the firepower available to both air forces it was surprising that this kind of thing did not happen more often.

Other RAF members, not leading so 'glamorous' a life as the fighter pilots, nevertheless were finding other aspects of life quite rewarding. George Belfield, an airman serving with the Parachute-and-Cable detachment at Brooklands, remembered this period of his life with a certain affection.

> "I used to court a couple of girls in the Byfleet area. Off-duty we'd walk round the outside of the track - they wouldn't let you cross the centre - and generally we'd finish up at the Sandpits. Local girls, RAF blokes, soldiers as well - the things that used to go on in those shelters were nobody's business!"

It must have been a wrench for the airmen when they were posted to Worth Matravers in 1942, although no doubt the maidens of Dorset were equally obliging. Perhaps there was something to be said for the blackout after all.

Chapter Eight

Through The Tunnel

The last month of 1940 passed fairly quietly in this part of Surrey. Although still busy, the Fire Brigade and Civil Defence Service could send some of their members to act as reinforcements elsewhere, to Twickenham, Southampton and Bristol. Although there were still plenty of alerts Göring's crews seemed content to direct their efforts elsewhere for the time being.

Over the Christmas period there was an unofficial truce. Three nights were free from raids, but heavy attacks resumed on London just before the year ended. Again the Weybridge guns fired at unseen targets, but if there were no successes for the gunners there were no bombs falling on them either.

A gunner's life was a hard one, for all sites had to be continually manned and the endless maintenance tasks meant that there was little sleep to be had between duties. The gun sites at Dunford Bridge, Woburn Park and Wisley Common were all on low-lying ground. It took time, with much argument between officers and civilian contractors, before enough hutted accommodation became available not only for the gunners, but for the airfield guards and the RAF balloon crews. In 1940 a gunner received just over two shillings (10p) a day, with only two free leave passes a year. Duty through the long cold night hours was loathed by all and there was the constant possibility of a move. In four years the heavy anti-aircraft regiments in the Weybridge area changed twelve times and the Bofors units fifteen times. The staff at Weybridge station became used to the sight of drab and grimy troop trains arriving at all hours to discharge heavily-laden men onto the platform.

Towards the end of 1940 a bulletin was issued to all ranks in Anti-Aircraft Command. 'Each time your unit moves, remember that you are doing it because it is the only way of defeating Hitler's constant changes of method, and a cold wet march will appear an adventure and not an imposition.'

What effect this had is unknown, but one move that was certainly for the better was the removal of guns and their fire-control instruments from Wisley Common to a new and drier site at Old Woking in January 1941. A new system of predicted fire was also being adopted and before long this would pay off.

The pace of operations seemed to have slackened, but there was still the distinctive uneven throb of unsynchronised engines in the distance, punctuated by the screech of bombs and the patter of falling shrapnel. Throughout Britain soldiers and civilians alike lived from day to day, sensing that if it was not their turn tonight then it could well be tomorrow.

31st January 1941

Balloon barrages above clouds could be used as signposts by friend and enemy alike. Just before 13.57 hours the airmen stood-to with their rifles as the sound of gunfire was heard overhead. They saw nothing, but the Site 16 balloon, in the St. George's Hill area, collected several new holes. What must have been the same bomber crew then dropped nine HE bombs, evidently using the balloons as a marker. However, the bombs missed Brooklands, falling in the woods south of Whiteley village and across Burhill golf course. There was no damage or casualties.

While Air Chief Marshal Dowding had anticipated the night raids and devoted much time to solving the problems of night fighting, most of the resources allotted to Fighter Command up to 1940 had to be concentrated on the development and use of the Spitfire and Hurricane by day. In 1939 there had been no purpose-designed night fighter available, and as a result two other aircraft had been hastily adapted for this role. The Bristol Blenheim, a twin-engined type originally used as a light day bomber, was by 1940 outclassed by both day and night, being too slow to catch some of the bombers it was supposed to shoot down. The Boulton Paul Defiant turret fighter, also too slow to survive by day, proved to be not much better. The Defiant had no forward-firing armament. One way a Defiant could hit its target was to approach from behind and engage in a difficult crossover manoeuvre, firing upwards into the fuselage or

Loading clips of 40mm ammunition into a Bofors gun of the 5th Anti-Aircraft Division, circa 1941. The dark-coloured box at the right rear is a predictor, which measured the altitude, speed and direction of the target. This is a posed shot, which would have been more convincing had the two gunlayers' seats been occupied!

(IWM H10014)

banking across the nose and aiming down at the cockpit. As the bomber's crew were unlikely to sit idly by while all this was going on, there was every reason to believe that the intended victim would take evasive action and either shake off its pursuer or else collide with it.

As if this was not bad enough, a less practical approach was for the Defiant to pass underneath the bomber and then slow down, so allowing the gunner to fire upwards at the bomber as it passed overhead. This of course assumed that the bomber's ventral gunner failed to see the Defiant below him. If he did see it, he would be presented with a sitting target.

Due to restricted forward and downward visibility the Spitfire proved unsuitable for night fighting. In this regard the Hurricane was better. Its broad-track undercarriage was more suited to landing on bumpy grass airfields at night, but its controls had not been designed with night flying in mind and its speed was reduced by exhaust shrouds, which had to be fitted if the pilot's night vision was not to be ruined. Much against his will, Dowding reassigned two Hurricane squadrons to a night role and some pilots shot down enemy aircraft by visual interception alone. However, the Hurricane could only be regarded as a stopgap. Despite the assistance given by the RDF stations, to be really sure of finding a target a night fighter had to carry its own radar, and the Hurricane's cramped cockpit could not be adapted for such a task. Airborne Interception sets - known simply as AI sets to those who used them - were fitted to some Blenheims and Defiants, but still their rate of success remained low.

In September 1940, as the night Blitz began in earnest, help came along in the shape of the Bristol Beaufighter. This tough looking bruiser of an aircraft, whose short nose and massive radial engines gave it a distinctively pugnacious look, was to prove a better night fighter, although not all aircrew liked it. Nicknamed the 'Beau' or 'two engines, hotly pursued by an airframe', it mounted four 20mm cannon beneath the nose and six 0.303 machine guns in the wings. This was more than sufficient firepower to blast anything in front of it out of the sky and it could carry an AI set in the rear fuselage, monitored by an observer, who directed the pilot towards his target.

This combination proved particularly successful in the hands of John Cunningham, a Beaufighter pilot who accounted for several bombers during this period. With AI secret and therefore censored, the Press dubbed Cunningham 'Cat's Eyes' and claimed that he possessed abnormal vision. It was a title that Cunningham and others in his squadron heartily loathed. While no-one doubted his skill as a pilot, like his lesser-known colleagues he depended on the skill of his AI operator, C F 'Jimmy' Rawnsley, and both relied on the ground controller to vector them onto the target. It was the pilot's thumb on the gun button, but the destruction of an enemy bomber at night was very much a team effort.

Although in the right place at the right time, the Beaufighter was not without its vices, one of which was the performance required to enter it. The pilot climbed a ladder through a hatch below the fuselage, then grasped a pair of parallel bars to swing his legs and body forward into his seat, being careful not to kick any of the instrument faces en route. Having accomplished this, he then raised the seat back and strapped himself in.

The observer's lot also left something to be desired. Besides having a crude and temperamental AI set to contend with, he also had the job of servicing the four cannon - and fitting fresh ammunition drums in the dark. This was not easy while wearing full flying kit, especially if the aircraft was jinking to avoid return fire! The Beaufighter was also very cold to fly in, the cockpit heating doing little more than char the pilot's right heel. On his command, 'Flash your weapon,' the AI set would be turned on, but it was not unknown for it to pack up altogether, emitting an awful smell. At this point the crew would either go home, or else the observer would live up to his name by providing the pilot with a second pair of eyes, looking out of the rear fuselage blister canopy. After all, seeing was believing!

The situation improved later, with better AI sets and cannon shells belted up in large tanks instead of drums, but at a time when they were most needed, the few available night fighters were the RAF's Achilles Heel. It says much for the crews that they achieved any success, but they could not prevent the Luftwaffe from inflicting heavy damage, particularly on London and its surrounding districts.

The experiences of 219 Squadron, based at Tangmere, were fairly typical. Originally declared operational on Blenheims in 1940, their only successes had been two bombers 'probably destroyed' by day over the North Sea. The first pages of the squadron's Operations Record Book reveal a string of misfortunes and frustrations, from fruitless pursuits of X-raids (where even the target could not be identified as hostile, let alone intercepted) to instances where the guns refused to work. A somewhat cynical diarist recorded that at the height of the Battle of Britain, when the day fighter squadrons were knocking down scores of Germans, all that one of 219's aircraft could do was to chase yet another X-raid 'with customary lack of success.'

One of the squadron's 'radio observers', as they were then known, was Sergeant M I Rickers. This was a new aircrew trade, and his introduction to it had been a curious one.

> "I was an AC1, a radio mechanic assigned to fit Lorenz - a blind-landing system - to the Beaufighters. This turned out to be a hopeless task and I was left with nothing to do. At that time there was a shortage of radio observers because, stupidly, you had to take the normal bomber observer's course - and the duties of an RO were quite different. Some of the radio mechanics were offered an acting rank of sergeant. We couldn't live in the sergeants' mess, but we flew operationally in this rank. I flew with the CO, Wing Commander Tom Pike, who was an absolute gentleman. I also remember Squadron Leader Little, a flight commander. He was a nice guy - he had his feet on the ground. Morale was low at the time, and the Beaufighter was a pig - the vibration was terrible. The AI Mark IV sets we had at this time weren't a lot of use either - they suffered from what we called 'squint'. The De Havilland Mosquito, which we had later on, was a better aircraft. Over at West Malling John Cunningham and his RO, Jimmy Rawnsley, had established a rapport and were pretty successful, but all that did was make us envious."

On 14th February 1941 219 Squadron received a visit from none other than Marshal of the RAF Lord Trenchard, who, it will be recalled, had won his wings at Brooklands before the First World War. An imposing man with a loud voice, Trenchard did his best to boost the squadron's sagging morale. The diarist noted,

> "The general course of the conversation was admitting that night fighting was a difficult proposition, and although we have had several disappointments which tended to make us downhearted, he urged us to keep going and he was confident that this unit would achieve success in the near future."

Neither the 'Father of the Royal Air Force' nor the aircrew he addressed could have known just how soon that success would come.

17/18th February 1941

On this evening the crews of *3/KGr606*, a former naval air unit with a mixture of *Luftwaffe* and *Kriegsmarine* personnel, were ordered to carry out harassing flights over London, as weather conditions did not allow a major attack. Among them was a four-man crew led by *Leutnant* Günther Hübner. They took off

The Members' Banking Hangar at Brooklands in 1941. Within the hangar can be seen a partially completed Wellington or Warwick. On the banking between the hangar and the bridge is netting, used to camouflage much of the track.
(BA Weybridge MP49481 via Brooklands Museum)

from Lanveoc-Poulmic airfield near Brest at 19.00 hours in a Dornier 17Z and passed close to the Channel Islands. After crossing the south coast near Brighton they dropped most of their load over London after sighting the unmistakable U-bend of the Thames around the Isle of Dogs. Attempts had been made to camouflage the Thames with a mixture of oil and coal dust. This was not as stupid an idea as it sounds, but it did not work on a tidal river. The oily dust peeled back like a skin and was washed to the sides, so highlighting this landmark instead of concealing it!

For almost three hours the Weybridge heavy guns were in action, firing a predicted barrage between 12,000 and 16,000 feet. At 20.16 hours a gun-laying predictor in the Weybridge area picked up Hübner's Dornier as it turned away from London at 13,500 feet. Plotted by five separate predictors and illuminated by clusters of searchlights at 20.27 hours, the height and course of this aircraft were passed on to Fighter Command.

At Tangmere 219 Squadron's 'A' Flight had been at readiness, and four Beaufighters were airborne in a creditably short space of time. Second to take off was Squadron Leader J.H. Little, with Sergeant Pyne as his observer. The weather was fairly clear, with nine to ten-tenths cloud at 5,000 feet. Above it the sky was lit only by the stars.

As he climbed away from Tangmere, Little was handed over to *Flintlock* - the code name for a ground control station based at Durrington in Sussex - and directed to the northeast. His target at this time was some four miles ahead of him. Shortly afterwards there came a correction.

> "Bandit at angels fifteen, now to the west. Vector thirty degrees to port."

Little obediently swung the Beaufighter round onto this new heading, and it was not long before he spotted his quarry. What follows is taken from the combat report compiled by him afterwards.

> "After being vectored thirty degrees to port I saw a pinpoint of light, on a converging course of about forty-five to fifty degrees, about 2,000 feet below. This light appeared to be exhaust flames. I asked control if it was an enemy aircraft and they confirmed it was. I told the operator to flash and proceeded to lose height and overtaking speed by S-turns behind the enemy aircraft. Although I kept the exhaust flames in view the whole time AI was of great assistance as a check......I opened fire at about two hundred yards, when flashes and sparks seemed to come from the port engine of the enemy aircraft."

Little's aim was true, but his fire had actually struck the Dornier's starboard engine, which burst into flames. Both Hübner's rear gunners had been trying to dump a box of incendiaries through a hatch at the time, and for this reason neither fired at the Beaufighter, or even saw it until it was too late. Little's attack came as a complete surprise, and the impact of his cannon shells filled the Dornier's cockpit with smoke.

Little continued,

> "I was blinded by flashes, the silhouette of the enemy aircraft being obscured, but continued to fire at the flashes until I judged myself to be

A well-worn Beaufighter If in flight. This one lacks the AI aerials that Squadron Leader Little's aircraft carried. (IWM E(MOS)353)

within fifty yards of the enemy aircraft. I ceased fire, eased the stick back and passed about ten feet above the enemy aircraft at an overtaking speed of about twenty miles an hour......I turned through 360 degrees after breaking away, but could see nothing except several incendiaries that showed through cloud."

Evidently Hübner's crew had finally got rid of the last of their load - not that it mattered now. He was unable to hold the Dornier on course, and as they began to lose height he saw Little's Beaufighter nearby. Hübner then told his crew to bale out, but found it all but impossible to follow them, for when he let go of the stick the aircraft went down completely out of control. Finally he got clear, but as the Dornier went into its final dive it narrowly missed his parachute. After surviving all this, Hübner broke his ankle on landing, and although he carried a pistol it served only as a souvenir for the Home Guard unit that took him and the others prisoner. The Dornier crashed at Oakley Court, near Bray, three miles from Windsor, and was destroyed.

Little and Pyne returned to Tangmere, touching down safely at 21.10 hours. Of the four aircraft that had been scrambled, theirs had been the only one to meet the enemy, and to them went the honour of achieving 219 Squadron's first confirmed AI-assisted kill. The squadron diarist now cheered up, writing,

> "This success, coming as it did, has had a noticeable tonic effect on the squadron throughout, after a long period of hard luck."

No doubt the tonic - and the gin to go with it - flowed freely when Little was awarded the Distinguished Flying Cross the following month.

Whatever its shortcomings, the Beaufighter began to take a toll of the night raiders, and it was active by day as well. Jan Jacobs vividly recalled seeing one chase a Ju88 across the sky over Brooklands, but he did not see the outcome of this engagement, nor could he recall the date. No doubt the Ju88's crew would have found this adversary a hard one to outrun or shake off. Günther Hübner, as he exchanged a hospital ward for the dull but safe confines of a prisoner-of-war camp, must have considered himself fortunate indeed, especially as both the Press and 219 Squadron's diarist had described him as having been killed in the crash. It was a mistake that had come all too close to being the truth.

On the ground there was still little for anyone to look forward to except another sleepless night under the stairs, in a damp Anderson or a smelly public shelter. The *Luftwaffe* added to the difficulties of the defenders by constantly switching their targets. Plymouth's city centre was laid waste in a series of raids, and Hull, an easy target on the east coast, suffered severely. The small-arms, vehicle and aircraft factories around Birmingham drew unwelcome attention, as did the docks of Liverpool. The fact of a city being bombed on a particular night did not guarantee immunity immediately afterwards, for often there would be a further attack the following night to stoke up the fires. It may have suited Churchill to proudly proclaim, 'London can take it!', but when he voiced this slogan in the East End the weary response was, 'It's us that have to take it, mate, not you.'

RAF airmen on leave were not always treated as heroes either. Guy Gibson, later to become well-known as the first leader of the dam-busting 617 Squadron, took refuge in a public shelter in the King's Cross area and a woman, seeing his uniform, belligerently demanded, 'Why aren't you up there fighting those bastards?' Gibson, who was also very aggressive, did just that by doing a tour as a Beaufighter pilot.

Exercises continued alongside the real thing, and enemy paratroops, cunningly disguised as white-capped Welsh Guardsmen, 'invaded' Brooklands one chilly February morning. The battle was all over by lunchtime and the motley local defence force, which consisted of Bofors gunners, Pioneer Corps guards, airmen and Home Guard units, was judged to have won this trial of strength!

19th March 1941

At 02.40 hours two HE bombs fell near the junction of Byfleet and Brooklands Roads, landing close to a pair of cottages and making craters thirty feet in diameter. The second one uprooted an oak tree, which remained upright despite being blown against another one. An unexploded bomb was reported, but a hole in the ground allegedly made by it was discounted as a false alarm by a Bomb Disposal squad. There was slight damage but no casualties.

7/8th April 1941

One 50-Kilo bomb fell in the Weybridge area at 01.10 hours, followed by four similar ones, and a dozen that failed to explode. The Dunford Bridge gun site went into action at 01.20 hours when a single raider attacked Fairoaks airfield near Woking. Around two hundred incendiaries were dropped, some of which destroyed three Tiger Moth biplanes inside a hangar. A Miles Magister trainer and a Vega Gull communications aircraft were quickly moved out and saved, although both were damaged. At 02.30 hours more incendiaries fell on nearby Chobham Common, setting fire to gorse and bracken. Three HE bombs also fell near Fairoaks, but did no damage.

19/20th April 1941

On this night there was a major attack on London, and at 02.20

hours one unexploded bomb fell in the Weybridge area. This was followed by six 250-Kilo bombs. After months of frustration the 109th Heavy Anti-Aircraft Regiment's gunners were finally successful when at 22.30 hours they shot down a Ju88A-5 of *1/KG76*, using the new system of predicted fire. This aircraft crashed at Slaughter Bridge, near Slinfold in Sussex - an appropriate name as none of its four crewmen survived. For some reason it was described in the records of Anti-Aircraft Command as 'the only night raider to cross southern England', but as the capital's ordeal lasted for seven hours this could hardly be true.

2/3rd May 1941

This time it was the turn of the Liverpool and Birkenhead area to receive a visit from the Luftwaffe. Again the predicted barrage system was in operation, paying off again as the Fairmile Common site shot down another Ju88A-5, this one being from *9/KG77*. This time all four crew members bailed out safely and the bomber crashed a quarter of a mile from the gun site at 00.58 hours. The pilot, *Oberleutnant* H Hempel, came down near the gun battery's command post and was quickly taken prisoner, as were the others.

During the rest of 1941 German night attacks on Britain gradually abated as the strength of the *Luftwaffe* was spread to cover other new fronts. The first shots in the North African campaign had already been exchanged the previous year, and Hitler's armies invaded the Soviet Union in June. As Britain's night fighter defences improved, so the gunners were often obliged to hold their fire in order not to compromise a successful interception. Raids became sporadic, and daylight visits by the Luftwaffe even rarer, although occasionally a solitary reconnaissance aircraft appeared.

12th December 1941

One Ju88 was glimpsed in cloud at 11.40 hours by the Dunford Bridge site, which fired three rounds at it without effect.

By May 1942, due to the continuing lack of enemy activity, Anti-Aircraft Command issued a revised order to the effect that only half the gun sites under a particular unit would need to be manned at any time, with the remainder of the gun detachments being placed on three minutes' notice. At this time things became a little hotter for some anti-aircraft units when a heavy RAF raid on the old city of Lübeck led Hitler to begin a series of 'reprisal' attacks. These would become known to the British public as the 'Baedeker Raids', for British cities of outstanding historical or architectural merit listed in the famous prewar travel guide were all singled out for *Luftwaffe* attention. However, this made little difference to the defenders of Weybridge, who by now could spend up to a month at a time on a gun site without firing a shot.

The middle years of the war passed slowly, although not uneventfully. Newspapers told of a string of battles in exotic places from the Pacific to the Arakan, and telegrams suddenly arrived, announcing death, wounds or imprisonment. Britain became an armed camp and Surrey's streets filled with the uniforms of a dozen different nations. Inevitably some people grumbled, saying that while one lot of foreign enemies had not succeeded in invading, others, by posing as friends, had done so!

In 1942 Hawkers left Brooklands to concentrate their fighter production at Langley in Buckinghamshire. Their former assembly shed became for a time the home of a series of strange experiments connected with a new bomb, which in May 1943 would breach two large dams in the Ruhr, the heart of German industry. Vickers also devoted their production line to improved versions of the Wellington and, also in 1943, the Warwick, which appeared not in its intended bomber role, but as a transport and air/sea rescue aircraft.

The air above Brooklands buzzed with visitors, including the de Havilland Mosquito light bombers of 618 Squadron, who flew in to receive modifications for another new weapon. This was Highball, a smaller version of the bouncing bomb and intended for use against German shipping, although in the event it saw no action. Around the airfield the anti-aircraft units changed constantly and the barrage balloon cables continued to take a small toll of friendly aircraft, although not always with fatal results.

The dispersal of component production from the Vickers factory, although a sound move in 1940, caused plenty of administrative headaches, and the fact of being moved from

Brooklands did not guarantee safety from the continuing effects of the bombing. George Roake and his tin shop colleagues were moved to, of all places, the Sound City film studios in the Walton area. The soundproofed buildings proved useful, however, enabling a film starring Margaret Lockwood to be made in one studio while the Vickers workers hammered away in another!

"I spent a long time over there. That's where I met my wife. She got called up and was a bit miserable - so was I, and we got courting! All our line here was spread out. The machine shop took all the machines out and the lorries used to come in there - we had all these bays. So our lorry used to go into Weybridge and then there was a big swop from our bay into another bay, so the parts either went into the stores or the electricians'. It was a big gathering point. We still had no roof on the top. Everything was covered with tarpaulins."

This was, of course, the Vickers factory.

"Right up in the top we had a big siren. When it went off it quivered the tea in your cup when you held it - so what it was doing outside I don't know! But there was no argument - you heard the siren and you had to get out!"

When not turning pieces of tin into aircraft components, George and his colleagues also had firewatching responsibilities at Sound City, and in the main works too.

"We used to have one area set up with bunks, so if it was my weekend on firewatch I would not only work, but I would sleep there overnight. We would sleep with our boots on, fully clothed, with tin hat and gas mask and any fire equipment beside us. We would sleep on the spot because of these little thermite bombs that they kept dropping all over. They didn't come down in ones, but about fifty or sixty at a time, and they would spread out. Explosives were put in them to keep us away. We used to have stirrup pumps. It was a two-action pump, pumping up and down, with buckets of water and spraying. The bombs used a sort of electron-aluminium-magnesium combination. It burned with a vivid white light......The Germans used to have parachute flares, and the heat from the thermite would keep these things suspended in the air.

"We did firewatching on a rota and it was organized by the Chief of the Fire Brigade. When I was at Sound City we had brick-built shelters, similar to the ones we had in the streets. Then in the morning we used to go into the big mansion, which is still over there now, and they used to set it up for us to have breakfast. We could have a wash and brush-up, have breakfast and start work at eight o'clock. What I liked to do was a full weekend if possible, then I was clear for a month."

Although less obvious than the main works by day, since most

A Hurricane IIc, fitted with 44-gallon long-range tanks, at Brooklands circa 1942. Wellingtons and Warwicks are parked in the distance and, just below the trees on the left, the camouflaged Members' Banking is just visible.
(BA Kingston Box 49 HG10, via Brooklands Museum)

of them retained the outward appearance of their prewar roles, the dispersed sites could still be hit by the occasional stray night-time bomb, and Sound City was no exception.

> "We lost four people to one bomb. At first they thought that only three were killed and not four."

The soundproofing consisted of asbestos and wire netting, much of which quickly descended if a bomb fell in the vicinity. On this occasion one of Sound City's first aiders had the unpleasant task of checking through the fallen asbestos, and found the fourth body beneath it.

Air raids would never again reach the frequency of the 1940-41 period, but occasional attacks would continue whenever sufficient forces could be mustered, and whenever Hitler chose to demand revenge for further Allied attacks on Germany. As July 1942 ended it was decided that the *Luftwaffe* would mount three attacks on consecutive nights against the Midlands.

27/28th July 1942

This was the first of those three raids. During the night four gun sites, three at Slough and one at Weybridge, were in action, although with nothing to show for their efforts.

In three nights the *Luftwaffe* lost sixteen aircraft - perhaps a third of their available strength then in northern Europe - and this latest initiative petered out as they conceded another round to the defenders. Apart from a brief skirmish one evening in August, things remained quiet at Weybridge throughout the rest of 1942.

17/18th January 1943

This was the first large-scale attack on London since 1941. Radar began to show plots over France at 19.45 hours, and two raids developed. The first wave consisted of thirty-five aircraft, which crossed the coast between Dungeness and Beachy Head. By 21.30 hours most had departed, but stragglers kept coming in for another hour. The second wave, of about forty aircraft, came in at 04.15 hours on a similar course to the first, and the all-clear had sounded by 06.00. On both occasions the Weybridge guns were in action, but there were no major incidents in Surrey.

3/4th March 1943

A scattered raid was mounted on London again. At 21.14 hours the Weybridge guns engaged the first wave of some thirty-five enemy aircraft, which this time had come in over Southwold. At around 04.00 hours a second wave of thirty aircraft attacked, coming in over Kent. Most of this wave concentrated on Biggin Hill and the Medway area, although one aircraft continued to Guildford, leaving via Horsham. This was fired on by the Weybridge defenders. Most of the bombs from the first wave fell in the London docks, but no major incidents were reported.

Until 1942 the Messerschmitt Bf109 had been the standard *Luftwaffe* fighter, but Fighter Command received a shock when the '109 was joined by a new radial-engined design, the Focke-Wulf FW190. From March 1942 these aircraft began attacking south coast towns in a series of hit- and-run raids. These tactics proved difficult to counter as the FW190s flew across the Channel at low-level, remaining below the coverage of the coastal radar chain until the last moment, by which time a warning to Fighter Command was often too late. They could therefore bomb or strafe and be out to sea again before an alert could be sounded.

Although its performance fell off above 20,000 feet, at lower altitudes the FW190 was faster and more manoeuvrable than the Spitfire Mark V. There was much concern at high level in the RAF, leading to the new and improved Mark IX. Meanwhile a bold plan by Captain Pinckney, a Commando officer, was drawn up. This involved the Vickers test pilot Jeffrey Quill, who would be dropped into France, get onto a Luftwaffe airfield, steal an FW190 and fly it home! By chance, on the day this plan was due to be presented to higher authority, 23rd June 1942, a strange event took place that probably disappointed Pinckney but must have greatly relieved Quill.

After shooting down a 310 Squadron Spitfire over Devon, *Oberleutnant* Arnim Faber of *III/JG2* flew north instead of south, mistook the Bristol Channel for the English one and landed his FW190, after a series of victory rolls, at RAF Pembrey in South Wales! Faber was quickly taken prisoner and his machine minutely examined, but for the time being the problem of its interception, especially at night, remained.

During the summer of 1942 a new fighter-bomber version of the FW190, the A-4/U8, entered service. This version was armed with two 20mm cannon in the wing roots and a 500-Kilo bomb on a centreline rack beneath the fuselage. In the spring of 1943 a new unit, *Schnellkampfgeschwader 10*, moved to the Amiens area of Occupied France, from which, equipped with the A-4/U8, it would operate night intruder missions over London and the southeast.

16/17th April 1943

Between 00.10 and 01.30 hours the first fighter-bomber attack on London by night took place. Thirteen aircraft, all of which were probably FW190s, covered a wide area from Essex to Hampshire.

Some of *SKG10's* aircraft evidently flew in over Gravesend as several discarded wing drop tanks were later found in that area.

There were scattered incidents and the Weybridge guns went into action.

A small target, the FW190's trace on a radar screen was less obvious than that of a twin-engined bomber, and RAF fighters made no claims on this night. However, their intended targets had a share of ill-fortune as well. To the astonishment of the staff at RAF West Malling in Kent, an FW190A-4/U8 landed there. Like *Oberleutnant* Faber, the pilot believed he had flown back across the Channel and reached a French airfield. He too was taken prisoner and his aircraft, which was intact, was subsequently flown by the RAF's Enemy Aircraft 'Circus' Flight. This unusual unit, nicknamed the 'Rafwaffe', was kept going by means of spares taken from other wrecked *Luftwaffe* aircraft, which were supplied to the RAF from Brooklands by Thomson and Taylor.

Shortly after the first FW190 had touched down at West Malling a second one, incredibly, did the same thing, and was still rolling along the ground when the pilot realized his error. As he tried to take off again he was shot up by an RAF Beaverette armoured car, and the fighter promptly burst into flames. The pilot staggered clear, broke free from a struggle with one of the crew of the armoured car and then ran straight into the arms of the Station Commander, who was none other than Wing Commander Peter Townsend, a noted Battle of Britain pilot. Despite his burns the pilot survived. Two other FW190s rounded off an unforgettable night by crashing nearby, killing one pilot. All were from *SKG10*.

This incident served to show that while the FW190 was a potent weapon in enemy hands, any aircraft was only as good as its pilot, and navigation of a single-seat fighter over blacked-out and hostile countryside was never an easy matter. It is not known whether any of these four aircraft had been the ones engaged over Weybridge, but if not then their more fortunate colleagues certainly had been.

20/21st April 1943

At 22.15 hours Raid 21H was plotted, and thought to be two FW190s. Making landfall at Sandgate, they flew across London and over the Uxbridge area. One bomb fell at Twickenham. The

An FW190 of 7 Staffel SKG 10 that landed in error at West Malling on the the night of April 16th 1943. This aircraft, W.Nr.47155 'Yellow H' landed at 01.10 hours, the pilot, Feldwebel O. Bechtold, being captured. (IWM CH18222)

other caused damage to houses and hangars at RAF Northolt. At 22.41 hours the Weybridge guns unsuccessfully engaged both intruders, who left via Bexhill on the south coast.

18/19th May 1943

Ten enemy aircraft, plotted as nine separate raids, attacked the London area, the first crossing the coast near Ramsgate at 22.30 hours. Then eight aircraft, six of which reached London, made landfall near Dover at 02.10 hours. Bombs were scattered over north and west London. One aircraft, Raid 9H, flew over London to the west and at 02.35 hours headed towards Brooklands, pursued by a Mosquito night fighter. The Weybridge guns stopped to give the Mosquito a chance, but for some reason it broke off its attack and the guns resumed fire at 02.42. At 03.05 hours they also fired at Raid 16H, which came in over Bradwell Bay in Essex and left via Guildford, their fire again being restricted by the presence of a Mosquito.

In addition the *Luftwaffe* despatched a few twin-engined bombers by day on 'pirate raids', using cloud cover to attack particular targets, especially aircraft factories. One was seen over the Weybridge area at 13.05 hours on the 19th and was briefly engaged by the Fairmile Common gun site. It was not brought down, but there was no attack on Brooklands.

19/20th June 1943

Shortly after midnight two fighter-bombers were reported coming in from the Dungeness area. One flew over London to Watford and back, while the other, plotted as Raid 155H and identified as an FW190, passed over Brooklands, running the gauntlet of the Weybridge anti-aircraft fire at 00.54 hours. The FW190 headed towards Guildford and dropped its bomb at the village of Worplesdon. At 01.16 hours a second wave of fighter-bombers attacked the southeast, but none reached Surrey this time. Again a lost FW190 from *SKG10* landed on the wrong airfield, this time at RAF Manston in Kent.

During July 1943 three of the four *Gruppen* of *SKG10* were rushed to the Mediterranean to reinforce German resistance to the Allied landings in Sicily. *I Gruppe*, however, continued to raid the London area by night until early in 1944. It was later to be disbanded following heavy losses during the Normandy campaign that summer.

18/19th October 1943

After a long period of quiet, between 22.30 and 23.30 hours some ten enemy aircraft attacked London and the southeast from two directions. Six approached London via the Thames estuary and four came up from the Beachy Head-Selsey Bill area. There were a few incidents in the London area, the Weybridge guns being in action at 23.07 and 23.12 hours.

19/20th October 1943

On this night strong winds and heavy rain kept many RAF night fighters from flying, but it seemed that some *Luftwaffe* pilots were not to be deterred. The diarist of 605 Squadron, whose intruder Mosquitoes remained on the ground at RAF Bradwell Bay, noted,

> "Gale enveloped us this evening and we carried out no operations. The Hun on the other hand did, and flying in such conditions we wished him luck."

At 22.15 hours six enemy aircraft appeared over the Seine Bay area, three of them reaching London. Two flew out over

The versatile De Havilland Mosquito, seen here in its night fighter rôle. The AI transmitter aerial can be seen on the nose and the receivers on the wings. (IWM E(MOS)516)

Colchester. The third, evidently flown by a bold and indeed a lucky pilot, ventured as far north as Luton.

There were some minor and scattered incidents. At Brooklands, 954 Squadron were alerted at 22.17 hours, but their balloons were grounded due to a strike by lightning. A short while later gunsites at Slough and Weybridge engaged the Luton pilot as he headed south, but were quickly ordered to stop as at least three night fighters entered the fray. One was a Mosquito of the RAF's Fighter Interception Unit, flown by Wing Commander Roderick Chisholm, a successful night fighter pilot. This aircraft, based at Ford in Sussex, had been one of two FIU Mosquitoes held at night readiness. Chisholm chased his target as far south as the Isle of Wight, but did not see it due to flying through a cloudy and moonless sky the whole time. Flight Lieutenant Cooke, his observer, found the contact on his AI set becoming confused with spurious echoes and, lacking any further assistance from the ground control stations, Chisholm broke off the hunt and returned to base.

Two other Mosquitoes from 29 Squadron, also based at Ford, fared no better. The first obtained a good AI contact but then overshot its target. This Mosquito, now afflicted by a failed radio, landed at West Malling. The second one returned to Ford with a faulty AI set, and their quarry flew home across the Channel, blissfully unaware of how fortunate he had been.

15/16th January 1944

At 19.10 hours the radar plot of the first of three aircraft, all of which were thought to be FW190s, was noted in the Amiens area. In total eight aircraft crossed the coast, the first at Hythe in Kent at 19.30 hours. Five reached London and Surrey, causing only minor incidents. This time the Weybridge guns stayed silent, although bombs were reported at Esher. By 20.16 hours the all-clear had sounded.

Irritating as these attacks were, they had little significance when compared with the massive Allied bomber offensive against German cities by day and night. The new year heralded further *Luftwaffe* attempts to mount 'reprisal' raids, with the few remaining bomber units attacking London and the south-east in an offensive codenamed *Operation Steinbock*, although it became known to the British public as the 'Baby *Blitz*'.

While the Germans had learned much from being on the receiving end of the Allied raids, leading to improvements in their own techniques of attack, they lacked a reliable four-engined aircraft capable of carrying a heavy bombload. Their newest bomber, the Heinkel He177, suffered alarmingly from engine fires, and most of their bomber units were compelled to soldier on with the less effective twin-engined Ju88s, Ju188s and Do217s. The Mosquito, a fast and versatile aircraft, had replaced the Beaufighter in many night fighter squadrons, and the AI set it carried was being constantly improved. In addition, the anti-aircraft defences had improved considerably, with the widespread use of gun-laying radar. The *Luftwaffe* made efforts to counter this by copying RAF Bomber Command's use of *Window*. This was the codename for silver strips of paper dropped from aircraft to 'blind' radar sets by producing a multitude of false echoes. Possibly this was the reason for the confusion on Flight Lieutenant Cooke's AI set the previous October. This simple weapon's effectiveness had been shown by the RAF's use of it during the devastating firestorm raid on Hamburg in July 1943.

A Dornier 217E, typical of the bombers used in 'Operation Steinbock' in early 1944. (IWM HU2704)

The air war at night had therefore changed a good deal since 1940. The consequences were that the *Steinbock* raids were intense, intermittent and of short duration. They served in the end only to indicate how far the striking power of the *Luftwaffe* had declined over the past three years.

As far as the Weybridge area is concerned, records for this period state only that four raids occurred between 22nd February and 15th March 1944. These were described as of greater intensity than anything previously experienced. Thirty HE bombs, eight phosphorus oil bombs and some 2,500 Kilo incendiaries fell in the district, causing fifteen deaths, thirteen serious and ten slight injuries. This brought the total number of locally recorded raids to fifty-eight. However, despite the lack of detailed Council records for the early months of 1944, some details can be gathered from other sources.

21/22nd January 1944

The new offensive opened with two waves of enemy aircraft over the southeast. The first, around sixty of them, came in over Kent, Sussex and Surrey after 20.40 hours. Thirteen raiders reached London, but there was no serious damage. From 04.19 hours a second wave of forty aircraft attacked London from Sussex and East Anglia. At 20.46 hours the Fairmile Common gun site was in action against three targets and the Dunford

Bridge site five, all at once. During the small hours both were in action against the second wave, engaging seven targets between them.

29th January 1944

Sixty enemy aircraft were plotted over France and the Low Countries at 19.55 hours and the alert sounded twenty minutes later. There were some minor incidents, most of them in the Thames estuary area, but at 20.20 hours both the Fairmile Common and Dunford Bridge sites were in action. One of their intended targets was probably the aircraft that unloaded four HE bombs over West Horsley, killing one person and injuring three others.

A feature of this campaign was the heavy use the *Luftwaffe* made of *Düppel* - their codename for the RAF's *Window* - and equally effective. Bomber crews were directed to release packets of it at intervals, but particularly when a strange scratching sound was heard over the intercom. This would indicate that they were being tracked by British ground or airborne radar. As a further counter-measure, *Neptun* tail-warning radar was carried by a number of aircraft and RAF night fighter crews were to discover that their 'customers', although greater in number, were now rather harder to catch than before.

3/4th February 1944

This night's attack occurred in two waves. The first began at 20.40 hours, when twenty-five enemy aircraft crossed the southeast coast, five of them reaching London ten minutes later. The resulting alert lasted until 21.37 hours. There were scattered incidents in the East End, Kent and Surrey, with the Fairmile Common site in action. The second wave attacked during the small hours, over East Anglia.

20/21st February 1944

This raid turned out to be another two-wave attack. At about 21.10 hours radar stations plotted eighty-two aircraft over France and Holland. Their tracks converged over the Thames estuary, most flying in over Kent or Essex. Twenty-five reached the London area and some flew on over Surrey before returning on a reciprocal course. One aircraft, plotted as Hostile 226, was engaged by the Fairmile Common site, and although they made no claim a Ju88, possibly this one, was brought down by anti-aircraft fire at Croydon. A second one was shot down into the sea off Whitstable and a Ju188 was the victim of a Mosquito crew over Essex. There were several incidents in London, but this time none in Surrey.

The second wave consisted of three aircraft, which crossed the coast near Hastings at 03.05 hours, reaching Kent and the south London area before returning. This time there were no interceptions.

22/23rd February 1944

A hundred and eighty-five *Luftwaffe* aircraft were despatched, of which a hundred and fifty reached southern England. Their targets included London and the Slough area. Opposition was provided by night fighters, some from as far away as Norfolk, and by the guns at Slough, Weybridge and Wokingham.

Due to gaps in the available British and German records, as well as the speed of events on this night, it has not been possible to describe all of them in chronological order. There are some questions for which answers are either non-existent or uncertain. What follows is compiled from Service records and from an account written by Doctor Alan E Pierce, who worked at the Weybridge Veterinary Laboratory at this time. Despite its title, the Laboratory was at Coombelands Farm, between Byfleet and Addlestone.

At around midnight clusters of flares were dropped over the Thames and drifted towards Weybridge, illuminating a starlit night to herald one of the worst raids this town would ever know. Fifteen HE bombs followed, killing fourteen people and injuring another eleven, one of whom died five days later. At 00.27 hours, two houses in Vale Road were hit, followed at 00.35 by three bombs that caused no casualties. Six minutes later ten bombs partly demolished a school in Baker Street and struck a house in Old Palace Road. Queens Road also suffered during this attack, as can be seen from the accompanying illustration. Down the road, Cobham was also hit at 00.28 by incendiaries, but fared better with four slight injuries. Finally, at 01.02 more incendiaries fell on Hersham, causing further damage and loss of livestock.

As they surveyed the wreckage next morning, most of the population of Weybridge did not know that while all this had been going on an entirely different type of bomb had made a quieter, but no less dramatic, arrival at the other side of Brooklands.

The German magnetic mine, first used in 1939 against British shipping, has already been mentioned. From September 1940 parachute mines had been deliberately dropped on Britain, to become known as 'land mines'. As more than half their weight consisted of explosive, they caused widespread blast and damage and, since they lacked the tail screamer fitted to other bombs, they arrived with little warning. It was fortunate for those on the receiving end that the mines proved unreliable, for it was noted that about half failed to explode on impact. Surrey's countryside was no stranger to these weapons, for during the first month of their use an unexploded mine had temporarily closed the railway line between Guildford and Clandon. During October 1940 another 'land mine' had closed the Guildford-Dorking line and the A25 main road at Gomshall, but the naval officer who checked it had found it to be a parachute flare! Until now, nothing resembling a mine had fallen close to Weybridge, but there was a first time for everything.

Doctor Pierce, who was a member of the Laboratory's Home Guard platoon, was on fire duty this night, patrolling the grounds. Suddenly, a German aircraft flew low overhead, diving and climbing as it was pursued by a night fighter. Describing himself in the third person, Doctor Pierce later wrote:

> "Tracer bullets flew across the sky from several bursts of machine-gun fire. There was a sudden loud 'swish' - then silence!
>
> "Picking himself up from the ground, he wondered at the explanation - but not for long. The next morning, the staff at Coombelands Farm were forbidden to approach the shed to feed the trichomonas experimental cattle. Lying half-buried in the soil beneath a tree, its parachute caught in the branches, was a land mine, lying adjacent to their shed. Was it an unexploded or delayed-action bomb?"

He had witnessed the arrived of a 1,000-kg *Sprengbombe* - a blast bomb that the *Luftwaffe* had begun to use at the beginning

With devastation behind them, members of the Weybridge Home Guard take a welcome break. They were involved in salvage work at Queens Road, Weybridge, after one of the 'Steinbock' raids of early 1944. (Elmbridge Museum 432. 1972/2)

of January. One of the first two to be dropped had fallen in the Westcott area, near Dorking, together with two conventional bombs. The resulting blast had wrecked several cottages, killing nine people and injuring a further sixteen.

The SB 1000 was not a mine, but was easily mistaken for one due to the six-foot parachute attached to one end. It was an odd-looking weapon and quite unlike anything that had preceded it. It was some six feet in length, flat-sided, oval in section and tapered at its lower end -the part that was intended to strike the ground first. There were only two aircraft that could carry it, one being the FW 190 and the other the twin-engined Me 410. Indeed, the SB 1000's shape was due to its being designed to fit the bomb bay of the Me 410. This aircraft could carry two internally, their parachutes being paid out as they were released. An FW 190 could carry one on its centreline bomb rack. Generally of rough finish and field grey in colour, the SB 1000 resembled a discarded drop-tank - a mistake that had been made by the Sussex Police and not realised until a Bomb Disposal unit had been called in!

This new bomb was thin-cased, with explosive making up 82% of its total weight, and Doctor Pierce owed his survival to it not having exploded when it hit the tree. Earlier mines had frequently snagged their parachutes on similar obstacles just before impact, posing nasty problems for the naval officers who had to deal with them. Those parachutes had, however, been much larger than those used on the SB 1000. Should it explode, all that would remain would be a few fragments of casing and scraps of artificial parachute silk.

Someone else who had used up one of his nine lives was John Pulford, an air raid warden, who had heard the bomb crash through the tree. He was on duty at a printing press across the river Bourne from the Laboratory. The press had become a Vickers dispersed site, with machine shop and toolroom facilities. The tree, with its deadly load, was just one hundred yards away.[5]

As the SB 1000 was a bomb, its disposal was usually the responsibility of the Royal Engineers. UXB reports were passed by the Police, ARP and military personnel to the North Kent and Surrey District headquarters at Oxted, which was part of the Army's South-Eastern Command. After verification by a civilian Bomb Reconnaissance Officer, the Civil Defence Regional Commissioner at this headquarters would allocate priorities to the reported incidents and pass appropriate orders to the officer commanding 2 Bomb Disposal Group, at Tunbridge Wells. The various companies under his command would then deploy their Sections as necessary. This latest air offensive meant that, as in 1940, there were never enough Sections to attend every incident promptly. The Coombelands bomb would have to take its turn in the queue with many others, especially as experience with SB 1000s elsewhere had shown that, if they landed and failed to explode, they could be left for the time being as delayed-action fuses were not fitted to them.

---

5. This story was passed to the author by Mr Pulford's grandson, who is today the Curator of Collections at the Brooklands Museum

By this stage of the war, due to the huge amount of unexploded ordnance being dealt with, Company records were little more than monthly totals of defused bombs and shells, with no information as to where they had been found. It has therefore not been possible to identify which 2 BD Group Section dealt with the Coombelands bomb. 12 Company at Horsham seem likely, but their War Diary lacks the entries for February 1944. What is known is that, despite its being given the highest priority, pressure of work elsewhere was such that this bomb could not be disposed of until the 24th.

The SB 1000 carried a short delay fuse - no more than a few seconds - connected to an impact switch on its tapered nose. This allowed it to function with the least possible penetration and it generally exploded on impact, leaving a shallow crater. Its thin casing and small parachute - which allowed it to fall faster than a mine - indicated that it was necessary to carry a fuse of this type to prevent the bomb from breaking up before detonation if it struck a hard target, such as a road surface. This meant that the complications found in the various types of mine fuses and their attendant booby traps would not be present here. Nevertheless, the Ministry of Home Security had decided, a month earlier, that when an SB 1000 was found all buildings within two hundred yards should be evacuated. It was for this reason that the Laboratory's cattle could not be fed next morning, and why a thousand Vickers employees were moved away from the printing works.

Due to the proximity of the Vickers site, the bomb had been classified as Category A. This indicated that it should be disposed of as soon as possible. For the same reason, it could not be detonated where it lay. Given the above comments on the fuse, it may be asked why this bomb had not exploded when it had half-buried itself on landing. This may have been due to the parachute catching on the branches and thus slowing the rate of descent, or it may not have properly armed before release - in this case, if it had been hastily dropped from low level while the bomber was evading a fighter. However, fuses were often produced under duress by workers in occupied Europe and it was not unknown for some to be sabotaged during assembly. Some officers owed their lives to this and one, on taking a fuse apart, had found a note inside. Written in Czech, it said, 'This is all we can do for you'.

Whatever the cause, the failure of the Coombelands bomb saved many lives and another incident on the same night underlined this. An SB 1000 had fallen on some fruit trees at Purley, in south London. It exploded while still twelve feet from the ground, damaging four houses in an area of blast that stretched over a quarter of a mile.

On the afternoon of the 24th, a Section was finally able to get to grips with the Coombelands bomb. While they did so, at 15.30 hours, 2 Bomb Disposal Group notified the Ministry of Home Security regarding the location of the bomb and the Vickers evacuation.

Now it was up to the Section officer and his men. The procedure was to isolate the fuse, cut a hole in the casing, then steam out the explosive filling, a mottled creamy-yellow compound comprising four different chemicals. Once this was completed, the fuse would be extracted by remote control. Although booby traps had been discounted, there was still a risk of the gaine - a booster charge between the fuse and the filling - exploding. This could have maimed anyone foolish enough to risk removing the fuse by hand.

At 16.25 hours it was time for another signal: 'My 1530. The UXB parabomb has now been removed by the BDS'. The Bomb Disposal Service. An apparently routine message, accompanied by the usual clusters of wartime initials. It is to be hoped that whoever carried it out was suitably rewarded, although it is a fact that the British Army has never been noted for garlanding its men with vast numbers of decorations.

So, who was responsible for it landing there? The *Luftwaffe* lost at least nine aircraft that night and for four of them there are few details. A check of night fighter squadron records indicates that actual German losses over Britain and on returning home were much higher, with some aircraft shot down into the Channel. Even on their return they were not safe, for 605 and 418 (RCAF) Squadrons' intruder Mosquitos had targeted a number of airfields from Stade to Cambrai, resulting in at least four more kills.

A Messerschmitt Me410 - almost certainly the aircraft type involved in the Coombelands incident. (IWM HU3019)

Despite this activity, it cannot be said that the fighter that Doctor Pierce saw definitely shot its intended victim down. Two Me 410s were brought down over southern England, but one was picked off by the Slough guns to crash at Radnage in Buckinghamshire. The second was downed by Squadron Leader Caldwell in a 96 Squadron Mosquito at Framfield in Sussex, after being intercepted over the Channel on the way in. A third was pounced on by a 418 (RCAF) Squadron crew while circling Coulommieres airfield. Flight Sergeant H.Wilson, having already claimed a 'damaged' at 01.50 hours, reported shooting this Me 410 down three minutes later, but this seems to have been nearly two hours after the Coombelands bomb had fallen.

However, it is probable that there was a connection with two other incidents that night. At 00.20 hours another SB 1000 fell on open ground near Dorking. A Mosquito of 85 Squadron, crewed by Flying Officers E.R.Hedgecoe and N.L.Bamford, had been scrambled from West Malling at 23.45. They climbed to 24,000 feet under the direction of Wartling ground control, near Hailsham in Sussex. Their target was to the northwest. Strangely, it was circling over south London.

Bamford's AI set picked up a contact at six miles, a trace on the screen that grew into an Me410 at 1,500 feet range. This aircraft's slim fuselage carried remotely-controlled machine-gun barbettes, which now fired a wild, short burst as it dived to 4,000 feet in a determined effort to escape.

Although Hedgecoe lost sight of his target as it passed through cloud, Bamford's directions enabled him to stay in contact. His quarry climbed to 7,000 feet, then began a shallow dive at an indicated airspeed of 330 mph. Bamford's commentary continued, but they did not see their quarry again until both aircraft were down to a thousand feet, with less than two hundred yards separating them. When dead astern, Hedgecoe fired his first burst, then two more. Several strikes were seen, followed by a bright flash. Then pieces fell away and the burning fighter-bomber plunged into the Channel south of Dungeness.

Hedgecoe's attack had begun fourteen minutes after the Dorking incident, so it is possible that his victim had dropped the first SB 1000, circled and released the second as it passed over Byfleet. No other Allied night fighter pilot reported meeting such an evasive opponent on that night and the evasive action carried out by the '410 certainly matched those witnessed by Doctor Pierce. Bamford received a DFC, as did Hedgecoe, two months later.

Flight Lieutenant Branse Burbridge, also from 85 Squadron, claimed another Me 410 off Dungeness at around the same time as Hedgecoe's combat. He first contacted his opponent head-on, then turned in behind it, pursuing it towards the south coast in a flat-out tail chase. From the speed of the enemy aircraft and the fact that only three '410s were lost this night, it is likely that his opponent was actually one of two FW 190s from *Schnellkampfgeschwader 10* that failed to return. While it seems likely that it was Hedgecoe who chased the Me 410 over Coombelands, it is not absolutely certain. Whoever they were, both were lucky to have avoided the Brooklands barrage balloon cables.

On a lighter note, a story often told by *Blitz* survivors was that if a mine or an SB 1000 could be safely defused, the parachute was apt to mysteriously disappear afterwards. Silk, even the artificial variety, was a prized commodity and many a wartime bride-to-be found that the raw material for her 'bottom drawer' had been supplied by the *Luftwaffe*. The parachute silk of the SB 1000 came in a variety of colours - red, green, blue and even pink were reported - and this must have led to some bright new fashions!

23/24th February 1944

At 21.18 hours a large mixed force of *Luftwaffe* bombers and fighter-bombers, some one hundred and sixty aircraft in all, appeared over northern France. Ninety crossed the British coast between Dover and Selsey Bill, the first at Beachy Head at 22.00. They spread out, covering a front from Kent to Hampshire, and fifteen reached London, which came under alert from 22.00 hours. A minute later the sirens sounded at Weybridge, with oil and other bombs falling close to the 954 Squadron headquarters, which was at 'Silverwood', a house on the Byfleet Road at Cobham. There were no casualties.

In what seemed like a re-run of the previous night's events, a large parachute was seen descending, this time by one of 954's corporals, who was on duty at Site 11. The description of the parachute made it too big for an SB 1000 and also ruled out a flare, which used one ten feet in diameter. A Dornier Do 217M-1 of *2./KG 2* was hit by heavy anti-aircraft fire over the west London area and, after its four-man crew had baled out, it flew on to land virtually intact at Cambridge. Perhaps the Weybridge gunners had been successful and the corporal had seen one of the crew. They were all captured, but there are no reports of any being taken prisoner in this area.

The location of Site 11 is not known, but since the 954 Squadron sites were grouped around Brooklands, and the parachute was seen descending in an easterly direction, it would probably have fallen either on St. George's Hill or beyond, in the Seven Hills Road area. If this time it really was a mine, as the size of the parachute suggested, there was no indication that it exploded. This would not be surprising, for in that area were plenty of trees for it to catch on. A further possibility was Silvermere Lake, in which it might have armed itself without exploding. Another job, perhaps, for some long-suffering naval officer.

Central London received the worst of this attack, although incidents arising from it were scattered across the southwest. The Weybridge gunners, now stationed only at Fairmile

Common and Dunford Bridge, were in action, but made no claims for the Do 217.

24/25th February 1944

One hundred and seventy aircraft were despatched to London, although only ninety crossed the coast. Mosquitoes of 29 Squadron had a particularly successful night, shooting down five of them, one of which was a Do217M of *3/KG2*.

Squadron Leader C Kirkland and Flying Officer Raspin were scrambled from Ford at 21.30 hours under the control of the Tangmere sector. Visibility was excellent, with no moon or cloud. They were directed to orbit '0' - a prearranged navigation beacon - at 19,000 feet, and did so for fifteen minutes. They then saw a searchlight intersection some fifteen miles away and for five minutes flew towards this to investigate. An aircraft had been illuminated and was flying northeast some 2,000 feet below. Kirkland corrected his course and began to rapidly narrow the distance between them, flying at an indicated air speed of 340 miles an hour. The Mosquito overshot its target on the port side and by the illumination given by the searchlights the crew identified the aircraft as a Do217. Kirkland turned away to port, then back towards the Dornier, which was now about three miles away from him and still held by the searchlights. By now his quarry was at 14,000 feet, and had evidently lost height in a vain effort to shake them off. Guided by Raspin's AI set, Kirkland closed in and fired a two-second burst from dead astern, seeing many strikes on the bomber's fuselage. He closed the range to eight hundred feet and fired a further three-second burst from dead astern. This time the Dornier's starboard engine burst into flames and it immediately went into a vertical dive with burning pieces flying off. At 21.56 hours this aircraft crashed at Parsonage Lane in the village of Westcott, near Dorking, hitting a house. Two crew members were killed and the other two bailed out injured. Seven bombs, which had been intended for London's docks, were found in the wreckage.

Other *Luftwaffe* crews were luckier, at least for the time being. At 22.00 hours incendiaries fell at Walton, causing one injury. Fifteen minutes later one HE bomb and yet more incendiaries landed at Hersham, but evidently on open ground as there were no casualties or damage.

1/2nd March 1944

A hundred and twenty aircraft were sent to London, but this time only ten were reported to have reached their target - a further indication of the strain on the remaining manpower resources of the *Luftwaffe*. Some bombs fell in Surrey but there were no major incidents. After this there was a break of nearly two weeks, with only a few minor incidents in southern England.

14/15th March 1944

After taking time off to regain their strength, the *Luftwaffe* mounted what was clearly their equivalent of an RAF 'maximum effort' raid. One hundred and eighty-seven aircraft were ordered to London, attacking in four waves from France, Belgium and Holland. A hundred and forty reached the capital, causing widespread although not significant damage, some of it in the Weybridge area.

At 22.14 hours a Mosquito of 96 Squadron, flown by Flight Lieutenant Norman Head and Flying Officer AC Andrews, took off from West Malling under the control of the Biggin Hill sector. Visibility was good, with eight-tenths cloud and a rising moon.

The Biggin Hill controller, Squadron Leader LeRougetel, ordered this aircraft to orbit beacon 'K' at 20,000 feet. A few minutes later Head was informed of the track of the incoming raiders. He was allowed to investigate a searchlight intersection and some flares being dropped on a vector of 120 degrees from his position. Finding nothing, he returned to orbit 'K' again, and by chance Andrews' AI set picked up a contact on an enemy aircraft flying west at 18,000 feet. The crew then saw what they took to be a Ju188, which was taking very violent evasive action. It was evidently flying at very high speed too, for the Mosquito closed the range only with difficulty.

Head fired a short burst from astern at eight hundred feet, which had no visible effect apart from causing his target to turn to port and dive. Despite this the Mosquito crew maintained visual contact as the bomber then climbed and turned to starboard in front of them. Head now fired another burst, this time at a closer range. Strikes were seen on the bomber's port wing and a large white flash of flame leapt from the port engine. As quickly as it had started this fire went out and the bomber went into an almost vertical dive, leaving a trail of sparks behind it. Its fate was not seen by the Mosquito crew, but according to the combat report submitted by 96 Squadron's Intelligence Officer the bomber 'lost height so rapidly that it appeared most unlikely control could be regained.'

The squadron was later told that this aircraft was a Ju88 which had crashed near Tonbridge, but this was not correct. The Tonbridge aircraft had been shot down by a Mosquito of 410 Squadron. Head's victim had been a Ju88A-4 of *6/KG30*, which came down at Blackbrook, on Holmwood Common, near Dorking, killing all four crew.

This night was to prove an eventful one for Head and Andrews. On returning to beacon 'K' they were taken over by the Sandwich sector, saw a Ju88 silhouetted against the moon and shot this down as well, probably into the sea off the Kent coast as it headed for home. Nine *Luftwaffe* bombers were lost that night, so it was no surprise that 96 Squadron's diarist was in a boyish and bloodthirsty frame of mind. 'Bags of fun tonight,' he declared. He then went on to describe Head's two victims, the only ones to be claimed by 96 Squadron that night. 'Otherwise no joy!!!!!!!'

It has already been mentioned that the *Luftwaffe* had begun to booby-trap incendiaries with explosive during 1940. January 1944 saw the first use over Britain of the purpose-designed *B2EZ* incendiary, which contained two ounces of penthrite or a similar high explosive. It ignited on impact and a separation charge blew the incendiary and explosive containers apart, igniting a delay fuse. This would detonate the explosive after a delay of up to seven-and-a-half minutes, which made fire-fighting even more dangerous and heavy damage inevitable. The resulting fire would therefore get a good hold, and fireman worked with hunched shoulders, since there was every chance of being hit by another salvo.

At 23.00 hours incendiaries fell on Walton, causing one injury. This was followed ten minutes later by more of the same at

Incendiaries explode in a suburban street. All in a night's work for the Fire Brigade, ARP and public alike. (IWM HU662)

Weybridge. There was considerable damage and two further casualties, one of which proved fatal. Other dangers were to become apparent nearby during the coming week, when two unexploded bombs were discovered at Cobham.

96 Squadron might be in a party mood, but there was no success for the Weybridge gunners. It was just as this offensive began to end that they would help in shooting down their last victim, but even then there would be no celebrations.

24/25th March 1944

Another raid on the London area was in progress on this night, although no incidents were reported in Surrey. RAF Bomber Command was also raiding Berlin with eight hundred and eleven aircraft, while a hundred and forty-seven older bombers, relegated to training duties, carried out a diversionary sweep west of Paris - a lighter duty, but not without risks. Among them was a Handley Page Halifax Mark II from 1659 Heavy

Conversion Unit at RAF Topcliffe in Yorkshire.

This night became known in Bomber Command as 'the night of the strong winds', for a north wind, which had not been forecast, affected both the main and the diversionary bomber forces. Even when it became known its full strength was not appreciated. The Halifax, captained by Flying Officer MS Little of the Royal Canadian Air Force, was blown over a hundred miles off course. As it returned at 23.00 hours it strayed over the west London area.

At Fairmile Common and Dunford Bridge the gunners of 183rd (Mixed) Heavy Anti-Aircraft Regiment fired at the enemy aircraft above, the two Weybridge sites being assisted by the Slough guns. Failing to show any recognition signal, the Halifax was shot down, crashing in flames at Lodge Farm, near Little Chalfont in Buckinghamshire. Flying Officer Little was killed and the other three injured crew members were taken to hospitals at Amersham and Watford. An inquiry was held, but as Little's crew had not identified themselves the gunners were exonerated.

Another incident later that evening clearly showed that enemy aircraft had also been over the Weybridge area. Again a Mosquito of the Fighter Interception Unit was involved. This development unit's aircraft were mostly the current RAF types, but some Fleet Air Arm aircraft were also evaluated by the FIU in the night fighter rôle. RAF and FAA personnel serving with this unit therefore had the chance to fly a variety of types that were not normally available to them. When this Mosquito was scrambled from Ford at 22.52 hours it was being flown by Lieutenant J A Armour of the Royal Marines, his AI operator being Lieutenant G L Davies of the Royal Navy. This aircraft climbed to orbit beacon 'P' at 20,000 feet and what followed is taken from the combat report later compiled by Lieutenant Armour.

> "At about 23.10 we got a contact at three miles at 10,000 feet, and followed it for about twenty minutes until we got a visual on a Mosquito and on the exhausts of another aircraft it was chasing. We therefore broke away and returned in the direction of the orbit beacon P. In that area we soon got another contact in the direction of a rather poor intersection of searchlights. Range was three and three-quarter miles, our height 17,000 feet, and the target, which was a lot below us, was heading for London from the

southwest. As we turned in behind him and closed the range, it was obvious that he was taking fairly violent evasive action.

"Losing height, we closed in rapidly and at about one thousand feet I saw the enemy aircraft's exhausts and at six hundred feet could pick out its silhouette. I throttled right back and passed about twenty feet under the enemy aircraft. I slid off to port, and as I came in again a searchlight illuminated both of us and I saw the crosses under his wings. As he peeled off abruptly to starboard I opened fire with a two-second burst from twenty degrees off at about three hundred feet range. I saw what I thought to be strikes in the rear portion of the fuselage and tail. I then gave him another three-second burst as he was going down very steeply, but I saw no results. The enemy aircraft's height was then about 14,000 feet. AI and visual contact were lost immediately, and although we searched for some time contact could not be regained. We landed at Ford at 0107."

This combat had taken place over the Weybridge area and the aircraft was identified as a Ju88. It may not have got away, for the fifteen aircraft lost by the *Luftwaffe* that night included two Ju88s of *KG54*, neither of which was found afterwards.

Perhaps that crew survived, but there was one bomber pilot whose fate was not in question. Flying Officer Little, of the unfortunate Halifax's crew, was buried at Brookwood Cemetery near Woking, in a large plot which today still contains the remains of many wartime Canadian aircrew. Below the RCAF crest on his headstone is an inscription which reads, 'He stayed with his ship, saved his crew, and a village. We are justly proud.'

A month later both the heavy guns and the Bofors detachments in the Weybridge area packed up and moved on, some going to the south coast, where they would soon distinguish themselves against a new form of aerial attack. At Brooklands 954 Squadron reverted to 'care and maintenance', and their balloons disappeared from the skies around the airfield.

D-Day came, and as a new front opened up in Normandy people all over Britain began to heave sighs of relief, thinking that at last the war might indeed be over by Christmas. They had come this far, so what else could Hitler do to them now?

That question was answered in the early hours of 16th June, when a strange spluttering noise, likened by some to that of a badly-maintained motorcycle, was heard over Surrey. Suddenly it stopped and a small dark aircraft plunged down onto Hanger

Hill near Weybridge, accompanied by a roar as a ton of high explosive detonated.

Delayed by technical problems, and by an RAF raid on a testing range at Peenemünde in the Baltic during 1943, Hitler's latest 'revenge' weapons - the V-1 flying bomb and the V-2 long-range rocket - had not been ready for use until now. Although not 'raiders', in the sense that they could not return home, these pilotless aircraft, as they were initially known, were a strange and fearful sight. To many people their arrival overhead was more ominous than that of the manned bombers, for once the V-1 was launched from its ramp an impersonal and unfeeling robot brain took over from the human one. Also, unlike the *Blitz*, the introduction of these unmanned weapons meant that bombardment could carry on around the clock. There would be no rest for the defenders during the day. It took time to get used to the peculiar noise and the eerie spectacle of a fast-moving light in the sky, which maintained a straight and level course regardless of fighter attacks or gunfire.

Mrs Katherine Bull, who had worked at the Weybridge Veterinary Laboratory until starting a family, was to find herself on the receiving end of the new weapon. To quote again from Doctor Pierce's account:

> "At this time the general public knew virtually nothing about flying bombs. In this state of ignorance, several staff members who saw a plane come down, seemingly in flames, and explode, assumed it was a German bomber. Indeed, some staff innocently travelled up to London the same day and were puzzled by frequent and unexplained explosions. If Weybridge was unlucky to receive this early flying bomb, Katherine Bull was doubly so. She had just collected her baby from the so-called bombproof shelter and was cooking breakfast, when the next moment she was on the floor, wounded, covered with rubble, broken glass and dust.
>
> "Katherine and her baby were both injured but both survived. On leaving the Weybridge District Hospital six weeks later she was presented with a two-inch piece of glass - a memento removed from her neck. We heard a lot about the moral strength of the population during wartime, but it was a sad reflection on mankind that when the Bulls were allowed back into their badly damaged house a week later, her husband's silver cups and small rugs etc. had all disappeared."

Mr Bull had been fire-watching in the city and so escaped the blast, but had returned home to find his family injured and his home half-demolished. However, this story had a curious sequel,

A V-1 flying bomb, photographed seconds after launching. With extensive use of slave labour, the Germans produced these formidable weapons at a cost of only £125 each. (IWM CL3433)

as this bomb was to assist another member of the veterinary staff, J. Deans Rankin, with his research. Doctor Pierce again:

"The bomb which nearly landed on the Bulls' house at Hangar Hill also brought down the ceiling of Rankin's bedroom at York House.

Mr Rankin was particularly fortunate as he was sleeping in it at the time!

"Investigating the cause of the explosion, Rankin was on the scene shortly after. He recorded a strange sensation - the air felt cold although it was a June morning. The grass and shrubs in the immediate area of blast were covered in hoar frost and all around were scattered yards of strong steel wire. This observation was to be useful in his diagnostic work at Weybridge in the coming months. In June and August 1944 cattle began to die for no apparent reason across the south of England and two carcases were eventually sent to Weybridge for bacteriological examination. George Slavin and Deans Rankin carried out a careful post-mortem and bacteriological examination of the various organs. When the heart was examined there was a six-inch piece of wire similar to that seen at the site of the Bulls' V-1 explosion.

"With the second cow, going straight to the heat, there was an identical piece of flying bomb wire. An adequate explanation was forthcoming for all Rankin's observations. Flying bombs were powered by a mixture of paraffin (kerosene) and oxygen, under high pressure. This was stored in a container encased in steel wire for added strength. When the bomb exploded, the cylinder burst, scattering lengths of wire over a large area and lowering the ambient temperature as the consequence of the adiabatic expansion to below freezing point. The cattle readily picked up small pieces of wire, which passed into the reticulum, penetrated the wall and pierced the heart."

As previously mentioned, Canadian troops had been stationed in Surrey since 1940. By now, many of them had moved to the south coast as part of the invasion build-up. On *D-Day*, their 3rd Infantry Division had stormed ashore in Normandy, eager to avange the losses suffered during the ill-fated Dieppe Raid of two years before. The *Luftwaffe* had rubbed salt into Canadian wounds by dropping propaganda leaflets over Surrey and Sussex. These had included photographs of burning landing craft, stranded Churchill tanks and clumps of battledress that had once been men.

Although two other Canadian divisions were on the point of crossing the Channel, their 1st Army's headquarters was still at Headley Court, near Leatherhead and the headquarters for those troops directly under its command was at High Ashurst, just to the south. Scattered across Surrey were a variety of rear area units, from vehicle workshops to mobile bath services. Among them, living under canvas in the Ashley Park area of Walton, was a unit that has not been identified but is known to used Universal Carriers. Nicknamed 'Bren Carriers' because of the well-known light machine gun that they had originally mounted, these light tracked vehicles had become a familiar sight as they clattered around the streets of Walton. Their headquarters was in a house in Silverdale Avenue.

Given the fighting spirit of the Canadians and some resentment felt by those who had missed the 'big day', it was not surprising that this unit should decide to mount its own defence against the flying bomb. It was at best an optimistic one, for although the Bren was a fine infantry weapon, its thirty-round magazine would be of little use in an anti-aircraft rôle. A 100-round drum that was tried seems not to have been entirely popular or effective. In any case, deflection shooting - aiming ahead of a moving target - required skill to be effective and some units appeared to have favoured the more basic 'hosepiping' method. Today's old soldiers may consider the use of 0.303" bullets against the V-1 as a desperate measure, but as far as this area was concerned there was nothing else available apart from the warnings of the firewatchers and the Observer Corps.

The Hangar Hill V-1 was the first of eighteen V-1s that would fall in the Walton and Weybridge district. The second was to approach Walton shortly after midnight on 18/19th June. Among those on the receiving end of it were two people who, for similar reasons, would never forget its arrival.

Mrs Joan Mansfield was a former Waaf, who had left the service to start a family. At this time she was at home at 6, Thames Street, with her two-month old baby daughter and her husband, a Hawker engineer. Mr Mansfield was also involved in fire duties during the week and, as a result, had been issued with a steel helmet, which his wife was to make good use of before the night was over. During that afternoon and evening, what seemed like a never-ending salvo of V-1s roared over Walton, as if this area had been singled out for special attention. Their unforgettable noise had earned them the name of 'doodlebugs'. Mrs Mansfield watched as they passed overhead

> "After all these years I can clearly remember the day the doodle bomb hit Walton. It was a Sunday, just another Sunday, with a slight difference. Bren Carriers, manned by Canadians, were patrolling the streets, waiting to have a crack at the bugs as they flew over, hitting targets in Weybridge, sadly with loss of life..... We thought we were lucky as the doodlebugs were now passing over us. We breathed a sigh of relief each time the horrid engine kept going. Some of them were dropping in the river. I can remember my landlady and myself cheering."

However, as Sunday night turned to Monday morning, Mrs Mansfield's mood changed.

> "We heard this horrid sound, plus the sound of firing. This was coming from the Bren guns."

Somehow, out of all the bombs that were to pass overhead, Mrs Mansfield appeared to have picked out the one that would fall closest to her family.

> "Earlier in the day, for some reason, I had cleared the cupboard under the stairs and I had put the pram inside it. By now we began to feel very worried, so I put the baby in the pram and covered her face with my steel helmet, my husband bending over both of us."

W H Askew, a shopkeeper in Bridge Street in Walton, was one

of four firewatchers - two men and two women - who saw five bright lights coming towards them from the south, accompanied by that chilling noise. Over at Ashley Park the Canadians opened fire and, coincidentally or otherwise, one light dived towards the firewatchers, who hurriedly took cover. Askew dived down in a covered passageway between two buildings.

Mrs Mansfield saw nothing of this, but the sound, and the sudden lack of it, was enough.

> "Suddenly the engine cut out. We clung to each other. There was an almighty bang, a crash and everything went black."

Most V-1s exploded just below the surface. This one struck the top of an eight-foot wall, in just about the worst position possible. The Askew family's shop and home were wrecked, as was a nearby store containing a hundred gallons of paraffin, which promptly caught fire. Mr Askew found himself in the middle of the road, where he wisely lay without moving until the debris had stopped falling. When he recovered sufficiently to look at his watch it was twenty-five minutes past midnight.

The firewatchers blew their whistles, but there was no answer from the nearby warden's post. The warden had survived unhurt, but his wife, with Mrs Askew and her two daughters, had been in a shelter that had been made up under the shop stairs. By means of a prearranged whistle code it became apparent that all four were still alive but unable to get out until the firewatchers moved masonry that was blocking the door. The family finally spent the rest of that night in an unoccupied shelter at a friend's home nearby - a sleepless experience, as the vibration from other falling V-1s could still be felt. Three more would land in the area on the 19th.

The blast from the Bridge Street V-1 had passed between two pubs, 'The Bear' and 'The George', both of which still stand today, the latter on the junction of Bridge and Thames Streets. The blast struck the Mansfield family's home, kicking in the front door, walls, windows and part of the roof. They had, however, survived in the same manner as the Askews.

> "The next thing I knew, somebody was moving the debris away from the cupboard door. I can remember crying with relief that we were all safe. If we had slept in our bed we would have been cut to pieces, as the glass was shattered in thousands of tiny bits."

The impact of a V-1 was usually devastating. This huge crater was left when one exploded at Cobham during 1944.
(Elmbridge Museum 123, 1989/4)

Now they too sought shelter elsewhere.

> "I had friends in Ashley Park, so we decided to go there for the rest of the night. By now the bombs were coming really fast and, as we pushed the pram through the streets, they seemed to be following us. My poor husband tried to calm me. I was convinced Hitler had put my name on a bomb and before the night was out I would be dead. We got to our friend's house in one piece, but there was more panic there. Mr Hembry was running all over the place looking for us. He finally spoke to somebody who told him that I had said I was going to Ashley Park. He told me that he was so happy that the baby and I were safe that he kissed the lady. The next day we heard that five people were killed that night."

As daylight came, the Askew family surveyed the wreckage of their home. Their baby's cot, which had been empty at the time of the bomb's arrival, hung suspended from one window. Covered in dirt from the night before, their chief desire was for a wash, but this would have to wait until a change of clothing could be salvaged. Their neighbours, who had come to Walton after being bombed out in Wandsworth, had paid a heavy price for not taking shelter, for three members of this family had died and the other two had suffered grave injuries. At the rear of the shop had been Drewitt's Court, a cul-de-sac entered from a turning off Bridge Street, in which there had been workshops, a car park and a row of cottages, all of which had been demolished. Nettlefolds Film Studio, which also stood nearby and had been used by Vickers as a dispersed wing assembly plant, had its roof ripped off. Thirty cars were destroyed, with a hundred chimneypots and almost every pane of glass in the town centre. Such was the destructive power of the V-1 when it exploded on the surface.

Finally the Askew family had their longed-for wash. It was a hard and basic time, when the simple things of life, so often taken for granted, gave the most pleasure. However, the father, like Ernest Babb at Vickers nearly four years before, was to be left with a permanent reminder of what had happened. When he finally removed his steel helmet he found that his hair had turned white overnight, and no amount of washing would change it back.

The Mansfields were unable to continue staying with their friends, for Mr Hembry was killed by another bomb on the 20th.

> "We couldn't stay in the house, so the lady opposite invited us to stay with her, but it was a very short stay. I hung some nappies on her line and she told me that she couldn't have things like that spoiling her view. In a flash I had the baby and my few belongings in the pram and I was on my way back to my bombed home.
>
> "As the back of the house was alright I set things out in the kitchen. I made up a bed in the shelter, with a wooden drawer for the baby to sleep in. I felt more than happy to be under my own roof, safe and sound, able to hang nappies up without some selfish person telling me what to do. The Council were wonderful in those days. They sorted out the roof, doing temporary repairs. At the same time they tried to talk me into leaving my home to go to the Church Hall and to stay there for a short while, but wild horses wouldn't make me leave home again..... My house was a mess, but I thanked God that we were safe. This sounds a bit selfish, but I was very young at the time and it was all a bit much for me."

At the time of writing, Joan Mansfield still lives at 6, Thames Street. The house shows no obvious scars now. Looking at it today it is indeed hard to believe that a ton of explosive once went off nearby. Perhaps houses in those days, and the people

---

6. Appendix 2 gives a full list of local V-1 incidents in 1944.

who lived in them, were a little tougher and more resilient than they are now.

Given the effort the Canadians put into defending Walton and other towns in the south of England, it was indeed appropriate that they, along with British troops of the 21st Army Group, would over-run the V-1 launching sites in the Pas de Calais as they pushed the Germans back into Belgium. However, before that could happen, those sites, and later specially adapted Heinkel 111 bombers, would loosc off as many bombs as they could.

Not all the V-1s reached their targets, even if they eluded the defences. Cyril Flint, a Vickers engineer, recalled one that flew up from Cobham towards Brooklands.

> "It exploded in mid-air and bits fell in the Cobham area. The third I can remember arrived in daylight. I lived at Shepperton then, and I can remember some tracer coming up at it from that area - it seemed likely to come in through my window. The bomb flew low over my house - the wife screamed, jumped out of bed and ran downstairs! I think it landed in the gravel pits at the rear of the house, but I don't remember it going off."

Indeed, not all of them did, despite the considerable impact of a dive into the ground. This presented the sorely-tried Bomb Disposal units with yet another nasty problem - that of trying to defuse the bomb's warhead while others snarled through the summer skies above. Cyril continued,

> "One landed at about three o'clock one Sunday morning at the top of Green Lane in Shepperton - it had been diverted by a barrage balloon cable. It damaged two hundred houses and wrecked one completely."

Some children, still thinking they would live forever, thrived on this new excitement. V-1 fragments became valued souvenirs, although some small boys found out the hard way that it was advisable not to touch them until they had cooled down! Peggy Millson, still at her warden's post in Weybridge, noticed a new street game at the height of these attacks. A dozen children of varying ages would line up at the edge of a side road and stand still as if waiting for the start of a race. As it turned out, they were, for when a V-1 came within earshot they would listen intently. When the bomb's engine stopped they shot forward as if catapulted, stopping only when the bang was heard. A cheer would then denote the winner, who had run the farthest in the time available.

Adults found this new menace less amusing, especially if the bomb's engine stopped just before it was due to pass overhead. Six people died and a hundred and thirty-seven were injured between 16th June and 29th August 1944, when the last V-1 to fall in this area landed in the grounds of Whiteley village.[6]

The V-1s were to prove a danger until the last one was shot down by anti-aircraft guns off Orfordness in the spring of 1945. Of the V-2 rockets that followed, none landed in this part of Surrey, although three were to fall at Leatherhead, Woking and Ashford, near Staines.

Launched from mobile sites in Holland, which RAF bombers found difficult to locate, the V-2 was an ancestor of the intercontinental ballistic missile, and indeed of the Soviet-built *Scuds* that would be used by Iraq in the Gulf War of 1991. It was not particularly accurate or reliable, and over half blew up en route, which was fortunate, as although they could be tracked by radar their speed made it impossible for the Allied defences to intercept them. The V-2 arrived so fast that all that was heard was an explosion at ground level, followed by a strange noise in the sky, resembling a faraway express train. They remained a threat until two months before the war's end, when the last one fell on Orpington in Kent.

Finally, on 8th May 1945 Germany surrendered unconditionally and Victory In Europe was declared. Some of the lights came back on again and total strangers danced together in streets throughout the country. At Eastcote Avenue in Walton the locals celebrated with a huge party and a bonfire. The war in the Far East carried on for a few more months, until Japan was subdued by a new and infinitely more deadly kind of bomb.

The rejoicing over, it was time to pick up the pieces and go back to work. Battle-weary men in ill-fitting striped 'demob' suits came home, seeking the civilian jobs they had long looked forward to; home to a severe housing shortage and to drab, seedy years in which the phrase, 'Don't you know there's a war on?' had been replaced by a resigned, 'Well, you know how difficult times are......' ARP disbanded and demolition of the public and private shelters began, although even today some Andersons linger on as tool-sheds or coal bunkers. German and

6. See Appendix II

A post-war photograph of the Brooklands site, showing how the Vickers works expanded to cover much of the track. The runway was built in 1951. (BA MP26508 via Brooklands Museum)

Italian prisoners, clad in chocolate-coloured battledress marked by distinctive coloured patches, were employed as farm labourers, the last one departing in 1948, and a party of Dutch schoolchildren was made welcome while their country was being rebuilt. It would be a long time before things could return to normal, although there was no question of them being the same as before the war.

And what of Brooklands, the reason for at least some Luftwaffe visits to this part of Surrey? By 1945 the racetrack was in a sorry and neglected state, built on in some parts and overgrown in others. When the time came to remove the camouflage netting from the track, the poles that had held it up were found to have taken root in the earth below the thin concrete surface. Removing them only resulted in further damage. A section of the Members' Banking has been preserved inside the present-day Brooklands Museum site, and circular scars can still be seen on it where the poles were sited. Alongside the track at this point, where it joins the top of the Finishing Straight, is the round base of an emergency water supply tank, although the Members' Banking hangar, which it was built to serve, was finally demolished in 1985.

Several pre-war racing marshals' refuges, apparently adapted as air raid shelters, remain at the sides of Members' Hill and on top of it are two towers, one of which mounted a Bofors gun until 1944. Alongside them are the original Restaurant buildings, which held the gun detachments for four years and at times provided space for 'Every Night Something Awful' concerts.

In the face of bitter protests from the surviving drivers, who had looked forward to using it again, the track's remains were sold to Vickers in 1946 and Brooklands became just another factory airfield. An area that had once known the roar of the racing car would in future play host to the whine of the turboprop and the shriek of the jet engine as first Vickers, then the British Aircraft Corporation and finally British Aerospace would struggle to maintain their positions as world leaders in the aviation industry. AV Roe, with whom this process can be said to have begun, returned to Brooklands in 1954 to unveil a plaque close to what remained of the Finishing Straight, commemorating his first involuntary flight of nearly fifty years before.

Despite Göring's attempts to destroy it, the aircraft industry at Weybridge survived and carried on until a decision was taken by British Aerospace in 1986 to close the factory. However, the postwar history of this site and its decline is not part of this book.

At Brooklands the past and present are inextricably mixed. A reminder of the wartime raids came on 14th February 1990 when two labourers, digging the foundations for a new warehouse on the modern industrial park at the Byfleet end of the track, found an SC250-Kilo bomb in the ground near the site of the Hawker shed, which by then had been demolished. Site security informed Addlestone Police, who evacuated several residents from nearby streets in Byfleet and contacted 33 Explosive Ordnance Disposal Regiment of the Royal Engineers.

This unit, based at Rochester in Kent, still clears up unexploded wartime souvenirs, and the team that dealt with the Brooklands bomb was led by Captain Laurence Quinn.

Although far better equipped than Lieutenant Patton and his wartime section had been, the latter-day sappers' treatment of this unexpected find also showed a certain degree of improvisation. After first drilling a hole in the bomb's casing and steaming out its explosive filling, they then slowly and carefully moved the bomb to the nearby runway with the aid of a forklift truck. This operation was carried out overnight. The bomb was finally rendered safe by a controlled explosion that blew out the fuse the next morning, so rendering harmless any booby trap it might have contained. Captain Quinn was later quoted as saying that it was one of the hardest jobs he had ever had to tackle. The remains of the bomb's casing were subsequently passed to Brooklands Museum and went on display at a wartime hangar built on the Finishing Straight.

Chapter Nine

The Last Bomb?

I included the 1990 Brooklands bomb in the knowledge that it was not likely to be the last as far as this part of Surrey was concerned. After that account had been written, but before it was published, came news of another incident.

On Thursday 14th October 1993, gravel extraction was in progress at Apps Court Farm, which was close to the Walton reservoirs and has already been mentioned in connection with other wartime events. An excavator driver uncovered a large metal object, but did not at first realise what he had found. He struck it several times, knocking away the tail, before he finally picked it up. Evidently not yet aware of how fortunate he had been, the driver then pushed his luck still further by using a screwdriver to knock mud away from the casing.

This was the situation when a Police sergeant arrived on the scene followed, once again, by a detachment from 33 EOD Regiment, this time from East Anglia and commanded by Major Beaumont.

The driver's find turned out to be a massive 1,000-kilo bomb, six feet in length, whose bulk had earned it the wartime nickname of 'Hermann', due to Göring's size. Hurst Road, which ran past the farm, was blocked at the junctions of Walton Road and Weston Avenue by the Police while attempts were made to defuse the weapon. The 'Hermann' came in three different versions. This one was the L type, containing TNT, wood meal and aluminium powder, the latter intended to double the blast effect when it exploded.

Opposite page: The 'Hermann' bomb, sitting in the excavator shovel, being examined by Captain Lardner of 33 EOD Regiment, prior to setting the initial explosive charge. (The 'Informer' 27172)

As the bomb still lay in the excavator bucket, it was necessary for one of the sappers to quickly learn how to drive this vehicle before further progress could be made. The fuse could not be removed and, as the bomb was judged too sensitive to be moved through a built-up area, a 'low order' detonation was attempted. This involved the placing of a small charge of explosive on the nose of the bomb, to split the casing and enable the filling to be extracted.

The explosion was timed for 16.45 hours, giving time for children at nearby Grovelands School to get home safely. As a further precaution, three hundred people were temporarily evacuated from their homes to Ambleside School in Walton. The Thames was also blocked off and an air exclusion order placed over the site. As things turned out, these measures were to prove fully justified, even though the first detonation caused only a partial fracture of the casing.

Major Beaumont explained to the *Esher News and Mail*, 'There is always a chance, when doing this low order technique, of it going up, in which case you get a very big bang'. He was proved right by the second detonation at 17.18 hours, which exploded the bomb. A cloud of gravel rose up to fly across the reservoirs, accompanied by shrapnel, which ploughed through nearby trees. It was found up to seven hundred yards from the site and was still warm two hours later.

The explosion shattered windows in Terrace Road and at the Apps Court Farm shop, which was barely 150 yards away. The earth shook as far as Thames Ditton and people in Esher High Street were under the impression that a lorry had crashed.

On Sunday, 7th November, I went to Apps Court Farm and in so doing I had one of those lucky breaks that occasionally come a writer's way. Hurst Road, the continuation of Terrace Road, ran alongside the Knights and Bessborough Reservoirs before passing through Molesey to Hampton Court. The farm was on a stretch of open land on the edge of Walton, next to the waterworks, which, as Appendix II shows, were themselves involved in the V-1 attacks during August 1944. At the entrance, by a cottage, was a new sign - a black, silver-nosed bomb with the caption 'Bombed but not beaten'. That over-used

The new sign outside the Apps Court Farm shop, reminiscent of many such signs seen during the Blitz. (S. Flower)

phrase 'The Dunkirk Spirit' was, it seemed, still alive and well here.

Despite the dire accounts in the Press of destruction, the Farm Shop, a yellow brick single-storey building, was still intact, although some of the windows on its south side had been boarded over. A notice chalked on a blackboard announced that the shop was temporarily closed, but that some of its wares had been moved out onto the patio. There were a few people about and by chance the first person I approached was Ted Cherett, whose daughter managed the shop.

While working for Airscrew Howden at Addlestone, Mr Cherett had lived in nearby Sandy Lane until he was called up into the Army in 1944. Having spent most of his life in this part of Walton, he proved a useful witness, indicating the gravel pit where the bomb had been found.

> "This one turned up in the pit, about a hundred and fifty yards away. You can see where the soil's been blackened. They were building up this other reservoir - building up banks for it. It looked like Brooklands, so a lot of bombs got dropped around here. I used to collect shrapnel - I've still got some. There was a stick of six dropped and only five went off. One completely blocked Terrace Road -I saw a small red sports car in it afterwards."

This was the incident of 1st November 1940.

> "A bungalow along the road got a lump of tarmac through its roof from that one. There was a line of semi-detached houses built for the water board and it was in line with the end one - that used to be the Victoria Laundry at the the time. It's the furthest one from here. Our house was in one of the spaces where the bombs fell."

I climbed an eight-foot high earth bank to look at the bomb crater from a distance. The pit was enormous, with the sandy soil clearly blackened at the far end. From the grass and nettles on it, the bank had been there for some time, but in spite of being situated between the bomb and the shop, it had not prevented most of the windows from being blown out. One pair had escaped damage, but they were of wired glass - the type used in fire doors. Curiously, the cottage, barely a hundred yards away and in open ground, had apparently escaped without a scratch. It served once again to show how unpredictable blast could be.

An article in the local *Informer* paper the previous weekend had mentioned the possibility of the Army returning to check the site again. Although there was no sign of them on the ground, I was intrigued to see an Army Westland Scout helicopter approach from over Knights Reservoir and circle the site three times before flying on.

Clearly the farm staff were determined to carry on, but I was sorry to hear the following year that damage to the shop had forced it to close, despite their insurers finally agreeing to meet a £43,000 repair bill. At first they tried to use a war damage clause to avoid the claim and the Ministry of Defence had also denied responsibility by saying 'You'll have to blame Adolf for that one'. In peace as in war, it is the ordinary citizen who pays.

I walked back along Terrace Road and found the houses much as Mr Cherett had described them. In one row was a pink-walled bungalow whose roof had been repaired with tiles of a different colour. Perhaps this was the one hit by the November 1940 bombing. Further on, at the end of a second row of nine semi-detached houses, stood a single one of older design. Could this be the former laundry Mr Cherett had mentioned? Indeed it was. Although boarded up, derelict and surrounded by rusting litter, there was still a flaking sign on the wall announcing, 'J. Warner. Victoria Hand Laundry. No machinery'.

Just beyond this, a new road led towards the Thames, but the presence of a traffic island hardly seemed to affect the manoeuvres of the Sunday afternoon drivers as they swept past. I thought of the red sports car that had abruptly dived under that road surface on another November night, long ago, and wondered what today's drivers would have said if anyone had told them that story. Two bombs, perhaps both dropped on the same night. One had functioned as intended. The other had lain, silent and deadly, for over half a century, waiting for someone to stumble across it.

It had been a three-mile trek from Hersham station, but it had paid off handsomely. The full story of the Apps court bomb and another eye-witness to add to the list. I smiled as I walked back into Walton, but that expression vanished as I saw a poster appealing on behalf of the British Legion. A black and white photograph showed men in wheelchairs, row upon row, as if in a cemetery, accompanied by the caption, 'Remember the dead, but don't forget the living'. I walked on in a more sober frame of mind.

At the time of writing, this is the most recent bomb to turn up in the Walton and Weybridge area, although it may not be the last. Shortly after the 1990 Brooklands bomb story reached the Press, a lady who had worked for Vickers told me that there were three others buried in the ground between the Flying Village and the post-war runway. She said they had been marked by three small metal 'stars' set into the concrete apron in front of the hangars. Today, this part of the site is owned by

Trafalgar Brooklands, a subsidiary of *Trafalgar House*, the property developers. The hangars and most of the other Flying Village buildings have been replaced by modern industrial ones. Should this company decide to carry out further development of the site, these bombs will no doubt come to light if they exist. It is quite likely that they do, for a lance-corporal from 33 EOD Regiment told me, when handing over the remains of the Hawker bomb,

> "We've never managed to recover an intact 250 - we've always had to blow them up. Hundreds of these things were dropped all over the London area and never properly accounted for at the time. That's why they're still being found. And they're still dangerous."

The Second World War may officially have ended, but the story continues.

Appendix I
Air Raid Warning Procedures

Before the Blitz began, a decision had been taken by Sir Kingsley Wood, the Air Minister. Air raid warnings would only be sounded when an attack on a district appeared probable to the Commander-in-Chief of RAF Fighter Command. Warnings would therefore be issued at the discretion of Air Chief Marshal Dowding, based on his experience of the *Luftwaffe* and its tactics. The sirens were for the public's benefit, as the defences would have been alerted beforehand. In October 1939 a system of colour-coded warnings, to be issued by telephone, was instituted as follows:

Colour	Meaning
'Yellow'	A preliminary caution. Raiders 22 minutes' flying time away.
'Red'	Action warning. Raiders 12 minutes' flying time away.
'Green'	Raiders passed out of a warning district.
'White'	Cancel the preliminary caution.

The yellow warning was deemed confidential and any precautions taken were to be unobtrusive. The red warning was to be treated in the same manner, but was to be circulated to more recipients. The list of priorities, in descending order, was Government departments, Service establishments, ARP, Police, fire stations and finally factories. If necessary, factory sirens would be sounded by arrangement with the local Police.

Clearly factory production would be seriously disrupted by a series of red warnings, particularly at night. Therefore in July 1940 a new colour, 'Purple', was proposed as a lights warning. On its receipt all lighting exempted from blackout restrictions was to be extinguished, but at this stage no further action, such as a public warning, would be given. If purple had not been preceded by yellow, then any measures taken as the result of a yellow warning - such as the call-out of defence personnel - were to be taken anyway. The green code would be discarded and white would now indicate that the raiders had passed. This new sequence came into being on 25th July, the day after the first daylight raid on Brooklands by a single Dornier 17.

So, during the Battle of Britain the likely sequence of daylight warnings would be yellow, red and then white. By night it would be yellow, followed by a two-minute pause if possible, then purple, red and white.

Generally the system worked well, but an element of risk had to be accepted. Enemy aircraft thought to be on reconnaissance might chose to bomb as well. In the event of a 'surprise plot' - a raider suddenly appearing on the Operations Room table as being inland - the sirens were to be sounded anyway, whether or not bombs had already fallen.

Appendix II

The V-1 Attacks in 1944

Date	Time	Location	Details
16th June	0650	Hanger Hill, Weybridge.	11 seriously and 24 slightly injured.
18th June	0025	Bridge Street, Walton.	3 dead, 4 seriously and 27 slightly injured.
19th June	0215	Hit an uncompleted reservoir at Molesey Road, Walton.	No casualties.
19th June	0633	Burhill golf course.	No casualties.
19th June	1835	Rydens Road, Walton.	1 dead, 3 seriously and 15 slightly injured.
23rd June	0842	Southwood Manor Farm Hersham.	5 slight injuries
28th June	0345	Foxwarren Park, Redhill Road	No casualties.
30th June	2352	Refuse dump at Apps Court, Walton.	2 slight injuries.
2nd July	1459	Burhill golf course.	1 slight injury.
4th July	2019	Tumbling Bay Weir, Walton.	2 dead, 1 seriously and 3 slightly injured.
12th July	1525	Open ground south-east of Weylands sewage works.	No casualties.
20th August	0631	Barker's Farm, Apps Court, Walton.	No casualties.
21st August	0235	Bridge Farm, Byfleet Road	No casualties.
21st August	1446	Foxholme Cottages, Byfleet Road.	2 slight injuries.
21st August	1447	Seven Hills Road, opposite Hill Farm Cottages.	No casualties.
21st August	1456	Apps Court sewage farm.	No casualties.
21st August	1950	Allotments near North Road, Hersham.	6 seriously and 32 slightly injured.
29th August	1137	Grounds of Whiteley village	1 slightly injured.

Appendix III
The Witnesses

Names, ranks and titles given here were those in use at the time of the events described. George Edwards, for example, was knighted after the war for his services to aviation, notably on the development of the Viscount airliner. Despite being sited on the edge of Brooklands airfield, the address for the Vickers factory was Weybridge, perhaps in order to avoid confusion with the nearby Hawker works.

Algy Allington, schoolboy, Weybridge.

W H Askew, shopkeeper and firewatcher, Walton.

Ernest Babb, fitter, Vickers-Armstrongs, Weybridge.

Gunner Thomas Barrett, 301 Battery, 98th Heavy Anti-Aircraft Regiment, Woburn Park, Addlestone.

R L Beauchamp, draughtsman, Thomson and Taylor, Brooklands.

George Belfield, airman, RAF Parachute-and-Cable detachment, Brooklands.

Fred Bint, apprentice, Hawker Aircraft Company, Brooklands.

Robbie Bolton, toolmaker, Vickers-Armstrongs, Weybridge.

Norman 'Spud' Boorer, stressman and Home Guard, Vickers-Armstrongs, Burhill.

Katherine Bull, housewife, Weybridge.

Ted Cherett, propeller maker, Airscrew Howden, Addlestone.

George Edwards, Experimental Department manager, Vickers-Armstrongs, Weybridge.

Cyril Flint, engineer, Vickers-Armstrongs, Weybridge.

Jan Jacobs, schoolboy, New Haw.

David James, stressman, Vickers-Armstrongs, Burhill.

A W 'Boyd' Kelly, ground engineer and Home Guard, Hawker Aircraft Company, Brooklands.

James Lomas, improver and Home Guard, Hawker Aircraft Company, Brooklands.

Joan Mansfield, housewife, Walton

Peggy Millson, air raid warden, Weybridge.

Lieutenant John M S Patton, 1st Battalion Royal Canadian Engineers, Boxhill.

Ted Petty, fitter and Home Guard, Vickers-Armstrongs, Weybridge.

Doctor Alan E Pierce, veterinary surgeon and Home Guard, Weybridge Veterinary Laboratory, Coombelands Farm, New Haw.

Sergeant M I Rickers RAFVR, radio observer, 219 Squadron, RAF Tangmere. (Later Flight Lieutenant.)

George Roake, tinsmith, Vickers-Armstrongs, Weybridge and Sound City, Walton.

Bill Vincent, electrician, Vickers-Armstrongs, Weybridge.

Sergeant Bill Wright, Home Guard, Vickers-Armstrongs, Weybridge.

Appendix IV

The Casualties

The total casualties for the Walton and Weybridge area between 1940 and 1944 were 119 dead, 232 seriously injured and 396 slightly injured.

4th September 1940

In terms of casualties the attack on Vickers was the biggest raid of all. Numbers of dead and wounded vary according to which aviation history is consulted, but the following figures, supplied from Council records compiled at the time and now held by Elmbridge Museum, seem reliable;

	Men	**Women**	
Killed	75	8	83
Seriously injured	169	7	176
Slightly injured	204	39	243
Total			**502**

Number of bombs dropped 1940-44

Excluding the eighteen V-1 attacks, 389 high explosive bombs and about 4,500 incendiaries were dropped. Many of the latter also contained a small quantity of explosive. Twenty-nine oil bombs also fell in the area.

Total number of raids

The Council records include two incidents in which no bombs were dropped, but there was an exchange of gunfire. There were fifty separate raids and incidents up to the end of 1940, four in the first part of 1941 and another four early in 1944. Taken with the eighteen V-1 attacks, this gives a total of seventy-six. My own research has since shown that there were many other occasions when raiders were overhead but no damage was done on the ground.

Glossary And Luftwaffe Units

Glossary

AA	Anti-aircraft
AC1	Aircraftman First Class
AFS	Auxiliary Fire Service
AI	Airborne Interception (radar carried by RAF night fighters)
AOC	Air Officer Commanding
ARP	Air Raid Precautions
ERA	English Racing Automobiles
HE	High Explosive
MBE	Medal of the British Empire
Mixed AA unit	An anti-aircraft unit made up of male Royal Artillery and female Auxiliary Territorial Service personnel
Plot	An indication of an enemy aircraft taken from a trace on the RDF screen or from Observer Corps reports, and then represented by a coloured wooden counter on the RAF operations room table
RDF	Radio Direction Finding - the original RAF codename for radar, at least until 1943
UXB	Unexploded bomb

LUFTWAFFE UNITS

The basic unit was the *Staffel* (Squadron), of up to fourteen aircraft. Three *Staffeln* formed a *Gruppe* (Wing), and three or more *Gruppen* a *Geschwader* (Group). Each *Geschwader* bore a number which was prefixed by a series of letters denoting its role, thus;

KG -	*Kampfgeschwader* (Bomber Group)
KGr -	*Kampfgruppe* (previously *Küstenfliegergruppe*, indicating a former naval air unit)
ZG -	*Zestörergeschwader* (Long-Range Fighter Group)

In front of this designation, a number in Roman numerals would indicate a *Gruppe*, and a number in Arabic numerals a *Staffel*, so that *I/ZG26* would mean an aircraft of the 1st *Gruppe* of *ZG26*, while *6/KG26* would mean an aircraft of the *6th Staffel* of *KG26*.

Specialist units

Erprobungsgruppe 210 - (Experimental Test Wing 210)
V(Z)/LG1 - Fifth (Destroyer) Wing of *Lehrgeschwader 1*
SKG 10 - *Schnellkampfgeschwader 10* (Fast Bomber Group)

Epr 210 and *SKG 10* were both employed in the operational development of various aircraft in fighter-bomber and intruder roles, the five separate *Gruppen* of *LG 1* each having different roles and equipment. *SKG 10* grew out of *Epr 210's* experiences in 1940, its aircraft acting as intruders and fighter-bombers by day and night.

Index